The Case for
STEM
Education

Challenges and Opportunities

D1611277

The Case for STEM Education

Challenges and Opportunities

Rodger W. Bybee

NSTApress

National Science Teachers Association

Arlington, Virginia

National Science Teachers Association

Claire Reinburg, Director
Jennifer Horak, Managing Editor
Andrew Cooke, Senior Editor
Wendy Rubin, Associate Editor
Amy America, Book Acquisitions Coordinator

ART AND DESIGN
Will Thomas Jr., Director

PRINTING AND PRODUCTION
Catherine Lorrain, Director

NATIONAL SCIENCE TEACHERS ASSOCIATION
David L. Evans, Executive Director
David Beacom, Publisher

ISBN 978-1-936959-25-9
eISBN 978-1-938946-92-9

NSTA is committed to publishing material that promotes the best in inquiry-based science education. However, conditions of actual use may vary, and the safety procedures and practices described in this book are intended to serve only as a guide. Additional precautionary measures may be required. NSTA and the authors do not warrant or represent that the procedures and practices in this book meet any safety code or standard of federal, state, or local regulations. NSTA and the authors disclaim any liability for personal injury or damage to property arising out of or relating to the use of this book, including any of the recommendations, instructions, or materials contained therein.

PERMISSIONS

Cataloging-in-Publication Data is available from the Library of Congress.

TABLE OF CONTENTS

PREFACE

All those who provide leadership in STEM education will find this book useful. No doubt you are beyond worrying about a precise definition of STEM because you use the acronym within the context of your work. So, you ask, what is the value of this book? The value can be found in two of the book's features. First, the early chapters explore the history and lessons of reform and explain contemporary STEM in an attempt to make its complexity clear. In this case, the book provides clarity about STEM and lessons for individuals at the state, district, and school levels.

Second, the book proposes ideas and a helpful process of strategic and even factual plans for those engaged in improving STEM education at various levels. The value of this book goes beyond clarifying discussions—it should be used to develop action plans for STEM education.

Those familiar with some of my earlier works—for example, *Reforming Science Education: Social Perspectives and Personal Reflections* (1993), *Achieving Scientific Literacy: From Purposes to Practices* (1997a), and *The Teaching of Science: 21st-Century Perspectives* (2010)—will recognize ideas, themes, and models from those publications. In many respects, the application of earlier ideas, themes, and models to the challenges and opportunities of STEM education represents the central theme of the book.

This book should be of interest to national and state policy makers interested in STEM education, state-level educators responsible for STEM initiatives, college and university faculty who educate future STEM teachers, local administrators who make decisions about district and school programs, and teachers who represent STEM disciplines.

Acknowledgments

I could not have developed the ideas in this book without the ideas and suggestions of many colleagues and friends. I express a deep and sincere appreciation to Harold Pratt, Mark St. John, and David Heil for our extended discussions during annual NSTA meetings. For their recommendations about technology and engineering education, I thank Greg Pearson, Kendall Starkweather, Mark Saunders, Karl Pister, and Cary Sneider. Celeste Pea provided background on the origins of the acronym STEM. Working on the Next Generation Science Standards has provided numerous opportunities to explore my ideas about STEM with Brett Moulding, Peter McClaren, Nicole Paulson, Rick Duschl, and Stephen Pruitt.

Robert Pletka, superintendent of Fullerton Unified School District, gave freely of his time and insights about a school administrator's role in STEM education. Jennifer Jeffries, associate vice president at California State University, San Marcos, and I had a long discussion

Preface

about supplemental instruction and STEM education. I must thank and acknowledge Mike Lindstrom, past executive director of SciMathMN, for several extended conversations and permission to use his models for STEM. These conversations occurred during a 2011 policy-maker briefing in Minnesota.

Being an advisor to the Hands-On Science Partnership has resulted in several opportunities to discuss my ideas about STEM education with publishers interested in seeing that teachers and students have materials and equipment central to learning science, technology, engineering, and mathematics. For these opportunities, I thank Chris Chopyak, Steve Alexander, and Kathy Workman.

Kimberly Jensen from the San Diego County Office of Education did an excellent job drafting several chapters and established a foundation for the book. The final drafts were completed by Byllee Simon, who continues to be my assistant for numerous projects and to whom I am deeply thankful for all she does to make any project the best it can be.

NSTA had the proposal for this book reviewed by very competent and experienced individuals. When the manuscript was near completion, NSTA had the draft reviewed. I took all the reviewers' suggestions seriously and the book is better for their recommendations. Here, I thank those reviewers: Greg Pearson, Kendall Starkweather, and Francis Cardo.

I express my appreciation to NSTA's Claire Reinburg, for her continued support of my work, and Wendy Rubin, for her careful editing of the final manuscript.

Finally, Kathryn Bess has been an inspiration for this work, a source of numerous ideas, and consistently a critical friend.

Rodger W. Bybee
Golden, Colorado
2013

INTRODUCTION

How I Became Interested in STEM Education

The problems I address in this book were initially encountered through a variety of education workshops, presentations, and endeavors. Educators commonly use the acronym for science, technology, engineering, and mathematics—STEM—in diverse ways. I was struck by the contrast of authoritative statements that lacked specificity concerning the meaning of STEM. For example, individuals would proclaim, "We have a STEM center," "Our state has a STEM advisory committee," or "The district has a STEM program." Although I understood the disciplines to which the acronym referred, there seemed to be a lack of clarity about the meaning of STEM in the different educational contexts. With time, use of the acronym *STEM* spread within the education community, and the need for a clarifying exploration of the term *STEM* increased.

My initial interest in use of the acronym STEM was reinforced on numerous occasions for more than a year. The problem regarding clarity and meaning seemed to grow worse as STEM went from an acronym communicating four disciplines to the use of *STEM* to describe K–12 education groups, initiatives, programs, or practices. At one level, for example, one hears policy makers proclaim the need to retain individuals in STEM-related careers. In the K–12 context, I heard science coordinators proclaim the need to improve STEM courses. For the latter, it was not clear what might be taught and learned in the STEM course. I began to look for and ask second and third questions: What is the STEM program in your district? What does your STEM advisory committee discuss? What is the work of your STEM center? It should come as no surprise that the answers were sincere but quite varied. *STEM* referred to whatever the individual or group was doing. Most often, *STEM* referred to either science or mathematics. Much less often did STEM address technology and engineering. When reference was made to technology, the term usually meant computers and a means of delivering instruction. Technology is greater than computers and more than a means of teaching.

During the period of engagement and observations about the acronym *STEM*, I worked on the science component of the Program for International Student Assessment (PISA). My work on PISA reinforced a long-standing conviction that K–12 education should contribute to individuals' life and work as citizens. Education in the STEM disciplines also should include the application of these knowledge, skills, and abilities to life situations in STEM-related categories such as health choices, environmental quality, and resource use. While understanding the concepts and processes of traditional disciplines certainly contributes to citizens' intellectual growth, I argue that future citizens need educational experiences that transcend the traditional

Introduction

boundaries of science, technology, engineering, and mathematics disciplines. It is not enough to assume that if students know enough biology, for example, they will make healthy choices. One argument in this book is simple and straightforward: If we want students to learn how to apply knowledge, their education experiences must involve them in both learning the knowledge of STEM disciplines and reacting to situations that require them to apply that knowledge in contexts appropriate to their age and stage of development. It really is not complicated. STEM initiatives have the potential to provide these educational opportunities.

To be clear, I fully realize that discipline-based knowledge is essential. However, so are opportunities to learn how to apply knowledge and skills to situations one confronts in life.

With time, these experiences led me to believe that the widespread and varied use of STEM, current discussions of reform, and long-standing aims of education deserved to be explored and, I hope, clarified in a book-length discussion of the challenges and opportunities of STEM education.

A Few Words About Definitions and STEM Education

As STEM education continues to expand and develop, use of the acronym has been applied to advertisements, classrooms, competitions, conferences, curriculum, resources, presentations, workshops, summer experiences, and videos, to name only a few examples. All of these examples present significant variations in what STEM education might mean and how it might be defined.

There is an interesting paradox I have observed concerning definitions in education: Many request a definition, and few agree with one when it is presented. So it is with STEM education. The meaning or significance of STEM is not clear and distinct. There is reference to four disciplines, but sometimes the meaning and emphasis only include one discipline. In some cases, the four disciplines are presumed to be separate but equal. Other definitions identify STEM education as an integration of the four disciplines.

In time, I have found it most useful to read or listen for the context within which STEM is being used. In a sense, the context clarifies the meaning of STEM. It may be four separate disciplines, as in "We need more individuals entering STEM careers," or a general category, such as "The teachers had STEM experiences in industries this past summer."

For the purposes of this book, I begin with these separate but related goals. Education should contribute to

- a STEM-literate society,
- a general workforce with 21st-century competencies, and
- an advanced research and development workforce focused on innovation.

The broader category, which applies to everyone, is STEM literacy, which refers to an individual's

- knowledge, attitudes, and skills to identify questions and problems in life situations, explain the natural and designed world, and draw evidence-based conclusions about STEM-related issues;

- understanding of the characteristic features of STEM disciplines as forms of human knowledge, inquiry, and design;
- awareness of how STEM disciplines shape our material, intellectual, and cultural environments; and
- willingness to engage in STEM-related issues and with the ideas of science, technology, engineering, and mathematics as a constructive, concerned, and reflective citizen.

This defines STEM literacy, a goal of STEM education. This goal has to be translated into policies, education programs, and, finally, the concrete practices of teaching. The contexts will vary as appropriate for formal and informal education; states, districts, and schools; K–12 and postsecondary education; and different grade levels, among other variables.

I hope the chapters in this book give direction to STEM education, if not a definition. That direction will be played out through leadership at the state, district, and school levels through policies, programs, and practices. To the degree this occurs, the education community will progress beyond Humpty Dumpty's view expressed to Alice in Lewis Carroll's *Through the Looking Glass*: "When I use a word,' Humpty Dumpty said in rather a scornful tone, 'it means just what I choose it to mean neither more or less'" (Carroll [1872] 1999, p. 57).

My Aims for This Book

My goals for those who read the book are to (1) develop an understanding of the historical and contemporary contexts of STEM reform and (2) provide some practical guidance and suggestions for STEM reforms that are appropriate to varied contexts—states, districts, schools, or classrooms. In addressing these aims, the book can be viewed in two parts. The first chapters present historical and contemporary contexts of STEM education. The latter chapters provide some practical suggestions as individuals become engaged in the reform of STEM education.

The first chapter discusses contemporary challenges of STEM education. The chapter describes several challenges and presents a model I introduced in earlier publications—the 4Ps of purpose, policy, programs, and practice—as a way to understand the various dimensions of STEM education. I return to this model in Chapter 10 and use it as a practical way to develop a plan of action for STEM education.

The second chapter reviews the Sputnik era and reforms of the STEM disciplines. The chapter includes the national mission and insights specific to educational reform. I include this historical discussion because Sputnik has been presented as a metaphor for the current era of education reform. This chapter is based on earlier work completed in 1998 while I was at the National Academies.

The third chapter sets the stage for the later chapters by describing several unique features for the STEM reform. The chapter addresses the themes of globalization and current STEM-

Introduction

related issues, 21st-century workforce skills, and the continuing pipeline of needs for scientists, engineers, computer scientists, health care workers, and other professionals.

Chapter 4 answers the question, How is STEM education reform different from other education reforms? The chapter discusses four themes as an answer to the question:

1. Addressing global challenges that citizens must understand
2. Changing perceptions of environmental and associated problems
3. Recognizing 21st-century workforce skills and
4. Continuing issues of national security

Chapter 5 provides an overview of 35 reports and articles that discuss STEM education. I have tried to move beyond the obvious point that STEM is used in many contexts with a variety of meanings and identify underlying and recurring themes that may be important.

Chapter 6 presents five policy recommendations for the federal government. This chapter is a response to a federal mandate to review STEM initiatives across federal agencies and coordinate, if not consolidate, various programs. This chapter provides an opportunity for me to make recommendations at the national level, as the remainder of the book addresses the state, district, and school levels.

Chapter 7 presents a framework and concrete way to begin thinking about STEM programs and practices.

Chapter 8 presents different perspectives of STEM education. I have heard or seen all of these perspectives, and it is highly likely there are more. These perspectives have been helpful to me, as they identify the meaning of STEM for those in leadership positions and certainly clarify discussions of policy and programs. My point is not to criticize or suggest one perspective. The idea is to help others recognize their perspective as they toil in the STEM fields.

Chapter 9 addresses a critical point that I have often heard. When taking a programmatic curricular view, does STEM imply an integrated perspective? Beginning with a view of separate STEM disciplines, the chapter progresses to a variety of ways that the STEM disciplines might be integrated. If you are thinking about an integrated approach to STEM, this chapter should help with the next steps and program design.

The final chapter will help you develop an action plan by considering critical factors such as the unit of change, resources, components, and support for STEM education. The plan should address the way you initiate, implement, bring to scale, and sustain STEM education, as well as how to evaluate the results. Finally, I return to the 4Ps and ask you to answer questions that help formulate specifics of an action plan for STEM education. Each chapter ends with several discussion questions for those conducting seminars, classes, or professional development workshops.

CHAPTER 1

What Are the Challenges for STEM Education?

If you are reading this sentence, you probably have an interest in STEM education. So, suppose you had to answer this question: What is STEM education? How would you answer? As you formulated the answer, what was the context of your viewpoint? Was it national policies, state standards and assessments, school programs, classroom practices, or something else?

As you answered the question, how did you think about STEM? Did you primarily think about a school discipline such as science or mathematics? Or did you consider four separate disciplines: science, technology, engineering, and mathematics? Or did you consider integrating two, three, or all four STEM disciplines?

Your point of view on STEM education quite likely was influenced by where you work, what you do, and your obligations. To state the obvious, the views individuals have of STEM education vary and are a function of their roles in the education system.

A FIRST LOOK AT STEM EDUCATION

Origins of STEM

Contemporary STEM originated in the 1990s at the National Science Foundation (NSF) as an acronym for science, technology, engineering, and mathematics. Here is a discussion I can imagine occurred. The first acronym proposed was SMET, representing the same disciplines but with an inescapable negative association with the word *smut*. So, the discussion continued with the question, "What acronym can we use for mathematics, engineering, technology, and science?" The answer was METS. Would this work? Then an insightful baseball fan responded, "No, that is a National League baseball team in New York." "Okay, how about STEM?" "Yes, that works." We will only have to worry about confusion with stem cell research. The acronym was subsequently used to describe various NSF initiatives and programs. STEM thus had quite a simple yet functional origin.

When STEM first appeared in education contexts, it caught the attention of several groups. Botanical scientists were elated, as they thought educators had finally realized the importance of a main part of plants. Technologists and engineers were excited because they thought it referred to a part of the watch. Wine connoisseurs also were enthusiastic, as they thought it referred to the slender support of a wine glass. Finally, political conservatives were worried because they thought it was a new educational emphasis supporting stem cell research. Actually, none of these perceptions of STEM meet the current use of the acronym for science, technology, engineering, and mathematics education.

The term *STEM education* is now widely used, but what does it mean, and how might it influence American education?

Confusion and Critics of STEM

A 2010 survey on the perception of STEM found that most professionals in STEM-related fields lacked an understanding of the acronym *STEM*. Most respondents linked the acronym to stem cell research or plants (Keefe 2010). Once again, the education community has embraced a slogan without really taking the time to clarify what the term might mean when applied beyond a general label. When most individuals use the term *STEM*, they mean whatever discipline they meant in the past. So *STEM* is usually interpreted to mean science or math. Seldom does it refer to technology or engineering, and this is an issue that must be remedied if STEM education is to have a positive influence on American education.

As STEM has become one of the newest slogans in education, some critics have noted its ubiquitous and ambiguous use (e.g., Angier 2010). Although the editorial by Natalie Angier accurately addresses a variety of issues, I contend the STEM train has left the station, and the challenge of stopping it and backing it into the station until there is consensus on the definition, meaning, and purpose is greater than trying to give directions and make constructive use of the term. One of the purposes of this book is to help individuals make sense of STEM education—in the context of their work—and move STEM from a slogan to a constructive innovation in American education.

THE CHALLENGES

Since its inception by the NSF, *STEM* has been used as a conglomerate term, not as an integrative expression. STEM describes general policies, primarily at the national and state levels. To date, neither a clear and definitive educational purpose nor implications for school programs' instructional practices have been systematically developed, especially in the context of pressing societal and global concerns.

Several things seem clear. The widespread depiction of STEM education is not really based on any definitive agreement of what the acronym means, beyond a vague reference to several related disciplines. The acronym *STEM* has political value for national and state policies, even if its meaning is not clear. Conversely, the ambiguous acronym *STEM* has little value when designing school programs and recommending instructional practices. STEM has potential for a significant innovation in education, one that could align with contemporary education standards and provide direction for crucial components of education reform.

STEM education presents several significant challenges. Use of the acronym and the associated ambiguity has served as a rallying point for policy makers and some educators. The power of STEM, however, diminishes quite rapidly as one moves away from national policies and toward the realization of STEM in state and local education programs. Let's examine some of the challenges.

The Challenge of Including Technology and Engineering

The first challenge involves actively including technology and engineering in school programs. Although one can identify technology and engineering programs, the scale at which they are in schools is generally quite low. Scaling up technology and engineering courses and appropriately including the *T* and *E* in science and mathematics education seem to be reasonable ways to meet this challenge. Note, however, that this approach maintains a "silo" orientation for the separate disciplines—that is, all four disciplines are represented separately.

Suggesting that technology and engineering be incorporated into one discipline, science education, is not new. *Science for All Americans* (AAAS 1989) and, subsequently, *Benchmarks for Science Literacy* (AAAS 1993) and the *National Science Education Standards* (NRC 1996) all included standards related to technology and engineering. For example, *Science for All Americans* set the stage with discussions such as "Engineering Combines Scientific Inquiry and Practical Views" and "The Essence of Engineering is Design Under Constraint" (AAAS 1989, pp. 40–41). In 1996, the *National Science Education Standards* included standards on science and technology for all grade levels, grouped as K–4, 5–8, and 9–12. One of the standards directly addressed the "abilities of technological design" as a complement to the abilities and understandings of scientific inquiry standards. In 2011, the NRC released a new framework for science education that included science and engineering practices (NRC 2011; Bybee 2011). Prior to these publications, the International Technology Education Association (ITEA; now known as the International Technology and Engineering Education Association) released *Standards for Technological Literacy* (ITEA 2000).

In addition, there are two significant initiatives supporting technology and engineering education. First, in March 2010, the National Assessment Governing Board (NAGB) approved framework for a national assessment of technology and engineering, scheduled for 2014. Second, the Next Generation Science Standards support these initial standards-based initiatives by including technology and engineering.

The Challenge of Using Contexts for STEM

One of the most significant challenges centers on introducing STEM-related issues such as energy efficiency, climate change, and hazard mitigation and developing the competencies to address the issues students will confront as citizens. Addressing this challenge requires an educational approach that first places life situations and global issues in a central position and uses the four disciplines of STEM to understand and address the problem. This has been referred to as *context-based science education* (Fensham 2009) and could easily be represented as a context-based STEM education.

The educational approach emphasizes competency in addressing situations, problems, or issues, and not exclusively knowledge of concepts and processes within the respective STEM disciplines.

The Challenge of Moving From STEM as a Slogan to an Education Definition

The many challenges of STEM education center on the fact that the acronym has been increasingly used and has reached a point where the ambiguous slogan requires definition with concrete and specific discussions in terms of educational realities. What, for example, does STEM mean for curricula, instruction, and assessment for states, schools, and classrooms? What are the implications for high school graduation? Teacher certification? State assessments?

In *Achieving Scientific Literacy: From Purposes to Practice* (Bybee 1997) and *The Teaching of Science: 21st-Century Perspectives* (Bybee 2010), I presented a model that I have found helpful in locating issues, initiatives, and approaches to education reform. The model uses the terms *purposes*, *policies*, *programs*, and *practices* to represent different education domains—in short, the 4Ps. I use the 4Ps in the following discussion of STEM education and in the process clarify my position and set the stage for later discussions.

STEM IS THE SLOGAN. DOES STEM EDUCATION HAVE A PURPOSE?

A definition of *purpose* includes synonyms such as *aims* or *goals*. Purpose is the object for which something exists or the goal toward which something strives. In contrast, a slogan is a phrase used in advertising, promotions, branding, or marketing. Currently, it seems STEM is more of a slogan than a goal-directed movement. As Israel Scheffler points out in *The Language of Education* (1960), a slogan serves as a rallying point and has key ideas and attitudes associated with it. To be sure, STEM has advocates and generates a sense of unity and common purpose. So, STEM as a slogan has value and is a rallying point. But with the passage of time (and I would note that more than a decade has passed), slogans will be interpreted by advocates and critics alike. In time, the slogan takes on a literal meaning that may or may not represent the movement's actual or best purpose. STEM now is seen in reference to a great number and variety of contexts and initiatives.

Why Clarify the Purpose of STEM Education

The term *purpose* refers to various goal statements of what STEM education should achieve, such as STEM literacy for all learners. The strength of purpose statements lies in their widespread acceptance and agreement among educators and their application to all components of STEM education. For example, individuals in the different places in the education system—such as teachers, curriculum developers, and and policy makers at the local, state, and national levels—would have general agreement on the aims of STEM education. Weaknesses of purpose statements exist in their ambiguity about the role of specific components of STEM education. For example, what does the purpose of achieving STEM literacy mean for an elementary-grade teacher? A high school technology teacher? A state STEM coordinator? A curriculum developer? A university teacher educator? Clearly, the answers vary. Individuals need statements clarifying the purpose of STEM education that are more concrete and related directly to various components of STEM education.

There is little need to argue that the purpose of STEM education is to develop the content and practices that characterize the respective STEM disciplines. Educators already have national standards, and some states have standards expressing these purposes.

A Proposed Purpose for STEM Education

I propose the purpose of STEM education is for all students to learn to apply basic content and practices of the STEM disciplines to situations they encounter in life. Specifically, STEM literacy refers to an individual's

- knowledge, attitudes, and skills to identify questions and problems in life situations, explain the natural and designed world, and draw evidence-based conclusions about STEM related-issues;
- understanding of the characteristic features of STEM disciplines as forms of human knowledge, inquiry, and design;
- awareness of how STEM disciplines shape our material, intellectual, and cultural environments; and
- willingness to engage in STEM-related issues and with the ideas of science, technology, engineering, and mathematics as a constructive, concerned, and reflective citizen.

Most educators would agree with this purpose but argue that simply learning the basics of science or math, for example, would result in students and future citizens developing the competencies to apply that knowledge to situations they encounter. Far too many counterexamples exist for this premise to hold. I argue that you must give students experiences in which they apply knowledge and skills if you want them to learn *how* to apply knowledge and skills. STEM education should address this challenge by providing students with experiences where they apply knowledge and skills to personally meaningful and socially relevant life situations.

GOT STEM EDUCATION POLICIES?

Policy statements are concrete translations of the purpose—for example, achieving STEM literacy for all learners—for various components of education. Documents that give direction and guidance but are not actual programs serve the purpose and give direction. Examples of policy documents include district syllabi for K–12 science classes; state curriculum frameworks; and national, state, and local standards. In the contemporary reform movement, there are some policies for STEM education, but it is safe to say they are not consistent at the national, state, and local levels.

Policies for STEM education would present conceptually and procedurally clear connections to the purpose for those charged with developing instructional materials and implementing teaching practices. The policies are like blueprints for a house. They express the architects' purposes and give direction to the contractors. Although they are not policies for STEM education, the new Common Core State Standards for English Language Arts and Literacy and Math, the Next Generation Science Standards, and technology standards for national and state levels all serve as examples of policy documents.

WHERE ARE THE STEM EDUCATION PROGRAMS?

STEM programs would be actual curriculum materials that exemplify purposes and policies. Although there are examples of STEM education programs (see, for example, NRC 2011; Hoachlander and Yanofsky 2011; Sanders 2009), the programs represent varied perspectives on STEM education. This is not unexpected, given the varied expressions of purpose and policy for STEM.

Characteristics of STEM Programs

STEM programs are unique to grade levels, disciplines, and components of the education system. They present a consistent, coordinated, and coherent approach to the STEM education of all students.

Development of STEM Programs

School STEM programs may be developed by national organizations, states, local school districts, or individual teachers. Who develops the materials is not the defining characteristic of STEM programs. That schools, colleges, state agencies, and national organizations have programs aligned with national, state, and local policies is the important feature and requirement of STEM programs.

SO, WHAT ABOUT CLASSROOM PRACTICES?

Practice refers to the specific processes of STEM teaching. The practices of STEM teaching include the personal dynamics between teachers and students and the interactions among students and assessments, educational technologies, laboratories, and myriad other teaching strategies.

Practices Should Be Consistent

The view of contemporary reform described here assumes that STEM teachers will implement classroom practices consistent with the policies, programs, and goal of STEM education.

Center on the Instructional Core

Improving the practices in the classroom center on the instructional core and the most individual, unique, and fundamental aspect of STEM education—the act of teaching students. From the teachers' perspectives, there should be little doubt about the need for local leadership and support for their work in contemporary STEM education.

WHAT ARE THE POSSIBILITIES FOR STEM EDUCATION?

If many policy makers and educators have assumed we need to improve STEM education and agreed to do something about it, then it seems important to have a map of the reform territory to know one's location, a means of movement, the direction of travel, what lies ahead, and a final destination. We can use the 4Ps model and themes just outlined—purpose, policy, program, and practice—for locating and clarifying different efforts in the geography of STEM reform (see Tables 1.1 and 1.2, pp. 8–10).

Identifying the Dimensions of a STEM Reform

The left column in Table 1.1 summarizes the perspectives of purpose, policy, program, and practices. The top row includes six aspects of educational reform: time, scale, space, duration, materials, and agreement. You can review the table and develop a general sense of the dimensions and difficulties of a reform effort as you ask questions such as the following:

- How long does it take to form STEM policies concerning standards or state curriculum framework?
- Once a STEM program is implemented, how long will it continue in a school system?
- Who is responsible for a particular effort, such as STEM curriculum, policy formation, or classroom practices?
- How do all dimensions of the framework contribute to the whole of STEM education?
- How does a framework relate to systemic initiatives?

Identifying the Costs, Risks, Constraints, and Benefits of STEM

Table 1.2 describes other aspects of a STEM reform. Again, the left column includes the 4Ps—perspectives of purpose, policy, program, and practice. The top row includes cost, constraints, responsibilities, and benefits and considers these in terms of school districts, school personnel, and students. The analysis presented in Table 1.2 indicates that although they are essential, purpose statements and policy documents have minimal and moderate influence on a STEM education reform. We are now approaching the phases in which risk, cost, constraints, personal responsibilities, and benefits are all high or extremely high. The STEM education clearly has significant challenges ahead.

Perhaps more important than the information in specific parts, Tables 1.1 and 1.2 give an overall picture of the reform effort. If I placed a "You are here" label on this map, it would be the interface between policy and program. We have some policies. The next phases of reform will take longer; involve more individuals, materials, and equipment; move closer to schools and classrooms; and present more difficulties when it comes to reaching agreement and actually implementing STEM programs and changing instructional practices.

CONCLUSION

Are there really challenges for STEM education? My conclusion is yes. Among the significant challenges, I would list the following: a lack of clarity relative to the acronym's meaning, the need to develop an educational definition of STEM, and the need to recognize technology and engineering as full members of the STEM quartet of disciplines.

Table 1.1. Dimensions of a STEM Education Reform

Perspectives	Time (How long does it take for the actual change to occur?)	Scale (How many individuals are involved?)	Space (What are the scope and location of the change activity?)	Duration (Once change has occurred, how long does it last in the education system?)	Materials (What are actual products of the activity?)	Agreement (How difficult is it to reach agreement among participants?)
Purpose	*1–2 years*	*Hundreds*	*National or global*	*Year*	*Articles and reports*	*Easy*
• Reform goals for STEM • Establish priorities for goals • Provide justification for goals	To publish a STEM document or place it on the Web	Philosophers and educators who write about aims and goals of STEM education	Publications and reports about STEM are disseminated widely.	New problems emerge, and new goals and priorities are proposed.	Relatively short publications, reports, and articles	Small number of reviewers and referees
Policy	*3–4 years*	*Thousands*	*National or state*	*Several years*	*Book or monograph*	*Difficult*
• Establish design criteria for STEM programs • Identify criteria for instruction • Develop frameworks for curriculum and instruction	To develop standards, frameworks, education requirements, legislation, and certification requirements	Policy analysts, legislators, supervisors, and reviewers	Policies focus on specific areas.	Once in place, policies are not changed easily.	Longer statements of rationale, content, and other aspects of reform	Political negotiations, trade-offs, and revisions

Perspectives	Time (How long does it take for the actual change to occur?)	Scale (How many individuals are involved?)	Space (What are the scope and location of the change activity?)	Duration (Once change has occurred, how long does it last in the education system?)	Materials (What are actual products of the activity?)	Agreement (How difficult is it to reach agreement among participants?)
Program • Develop materials or adopt a program • Implement the program	*3–6 years* To develop a complete STEM education program	*Tens of thousands* Developers, field-test teachers, students, textbook publishers, and software developers	*Local or school* Adoption committees	*Decades* Once developed or adopted, school programs last for extended periods of time.	*Books and courseware* Usually several books for students and teachers	*Very difficult* Many factions, barriers, and requirements
Practices • Change teaching strategies • Adapt materials to unique needs of schools and students	*7–10 years* To complete implementation and staff development for STEM initiatives	*Millions* National, state, and local educators, school boards, and the public	*Classrooms* Individual teachers	*Several decades* Individual teaching practices often last a professional lifetime.	*Complete system* Books plus materials, equipment, software, and support	*Extraordinarily difficult* Unique needs, practices, and beliefs of education leaders, school administrators, classroom teachers, and communities

Table 1.2. Cost, Risks, and Benefits of a STEM Education Reform

Perspectives	What is the risk to states and school systems?	How much will it cost states and school systems in financial terms?	What are the constraints against reform for states and school systems?	Who has the responsibility for reform at the state and school levels?	What are the benefits to states, schools, and students?
Purpose • Reform goals • Establish priorities for goals	Minimal	Minimal	Minimal	Minimal	Minimal
Policy • Establish design criteria • Identify criteria for instruction • Develop frameworks for curriculum and instruction	Moderate	Moderate	Moderate	Moderate	Moderate
Program • Develop materials or adopting a program • Implement the program	High	High	High	High	High
Practices • Change teaching strategies • Adapt materials to unique needs of schools and students	Extremely high	Extremely high	Extremely high	Extremely high	Extremely high

This chapter described different dimensions of STEM education relative to educational purposes, policies, programs, and practices. Using the 4Ps helps clarify different educational dimensions and the costs, risks, benefits, constraints, and responsibilities for STEM education reform.

The challenges of STEM education are many and varied. In the following chapters, I provide perspectives on what STEM education means and try to address some of the challenges. Specifically, the chapters

- place the STEM education reform in the context of other historical reforms, in particular the Sputnik era;
- clarify some unique aspects of STEM education based on a variety of reports and critiques;
- identify different perspectives of STEM in school programs and practices;
- present some alternatives that complement contemporary school programs; and
- provide processes to develop action plans for STEM education.

DISCUSSION QUESTIONS

1. How would you define STEM education?

2. Why does the acronym *STEM* work for policy discussions, yet present challenges for education programs and classroom practices?

3. What are the 4Ps, and how do they apply to the challenges of STEM education?

CHAPTER 2

What Can We Learn From the Original Sputnik Moment?

The term *Sputnik* has come to symbolize reform of STEM education and a response to a perceived national crisis. For example, some call for a Sputnik Summit to address the potential decline of U.S. competitiveness. Others simply proclaim the need for another Sputnik to initiate the improvement of STEM education.

The use of Sputnik as a metaphor reached its apogee in the 2011 State of the Union address to Congress, when President Barack Obama said to the nation, "This is our generation's Sputnik moment." Elements of this discussion are based on an earlier discussion during the symposium Reflecting on Sputnik: Linking the Past, Present, and Future of Educational Reform (Bybee 1997b). Because of the continuous reference to Sputnik, I provide some reflections on that historically important era in STEM education.

The thesis of this chapter is that Sputnik provides some insights and lessons not often discussed in the zeal to improve STEM education. The central discussion explores several dimensions and dynamics that influence present-day initiatives.

Those interested in detailed and thorough discussions of the Sputnik era would benefit from the following resources: John Rudolph's *Scientists in the Classroom: The Cold War Reconstruction of American Science Education* (2002), George DeBoer's *A History of Ideas in Science Education: Implementation or Practice* (1991), and J. Myron Atkin and Paul Black's *Inside Science Education Reform: A History of Curricular and Policy Change* (2003).

THE BEGINNINGS OF REFORM

The education reform of the 1950s and the 1960s was already in progress when the Soviet Union placed Sputnik in orbit. In 1951, with the leadership of Max Beberman (1958), the University of Illinois Committee of School Mathematics (UICSM) initiated a reform of the secondary school mathematics curriculum. In science, the stage had been set by Jerrold Zacharias, who in 1956 began the Physical Science Study Committee (PSSC) a year before the launch of Sputnik. However, Sputnik still played a significant role in the educational reform of this era.

A Turning Point in the History of Education

The Sputnik era was a significant turning point for the STEM disciplines. It brought the sciences and mathematics to the foreground of education reform, but unfortunately it also moved technology and engineering to the background. There is no small amount of irony in this, as a goal of the Sputnik era was sending men to the Moon. One of the great engineering and technological accomplishments in history was achieved while technology and engineering were explicitly downplayed in STEM education.

For the public, Sputnik symbolized a threat to American security, our superiority in science and math, and our economic progress and political freedom. In short, because of Sputnik, the United States perceived itself as scientifically, technologically, militarily, and economically weak. As a result, educators, scientists, and mathematicians broadened and accelerated education reform, the public understood and supported the effort, and policy makers increased federal funding.

Programs as the Means of Reform

The Sputnik era for science, technology, engineering, and mathematics education began in the 1950s with the development of new programs that eventually became known by their acronyms. Science programs included PSSC Physics; the Chemical Education Materials Study, known as CHEM Study; the Chemical Bond Approach, known as CBA; the Biological Sciences Curriculum Study, known as BSCS biology; and the Earth Science Curriculum Project, known as ESCP Earth science. At the elementary level, there was the Elementary Science Study, known as ESS; the Science Curriculum Improvement Study, known as SCIS; Science-A Process Approach, known as S-APA, and Conceptually Oriented Program in Elementary Science, known as COPES.

In mathematics, the programs included UICSM, the School Mathematics Study Group (SMSG), the Greater Cleveland Mathematics Program (GCMP), the University of Illinois Arithmetic Project, the University of Maryland Mathematics Project (UMMaP), the Suppes Experimental Project in the Teaching of Elementary-School Mathematics, and the Madison Project.

Technology and engineering had only a minor and late entry: the Engineering Concepts Curriculum Project (ECCP), which began in 1965 and published a program titled *The Man Made World* in 1971.

WHAT WAS EDUCATION LIKE BEFORE SPUTNIK?

After World War II, debate about the quality of American education escalated. Individuals such as Admiral Hyman Rickover, and most notably Arthur Bestor, became critics of John Dewey's ideas and progressive education, especially the theme of life adjustment. The dominant theme of the critics was *back*—back to fundamentals, back to basics, back to drill and memorization, and back to facts. Bestor called for a return to past practices and argued for a restoration of learning as the theme for reform (Cremin 1961; Ravitch 1983).

Criticizing Education Reforms

Several observations are worth noting about the criticism of progressive ideas and emergence of Sputnik-spurred programs. First, such criticisms were not new; for example, in the late 1800s, critics said that students were being spoon-fed, the curriculum was too easy, and music and art took too much time from fundamentals. Second, some of what critics wrote included a serious distortion of facts. Furthermore, the critics seldom appealed to evidence in support of their arguments; they relied on personal opinion and powerful rhetoric. Third, educators did not respond to the critics. There is no clear explanation for the educators' silence. Recall, however, that this was the Cold War and the period of McCarthyism, so they may have been fearful to say anything. Also, progressive education was on the decline. In 1955, the Progressive Education Association closed its doors, and the journal *Progressive Education* ceased publishing two years later. So, those disposed to counter the critics may have thought it would make no difference. Regardless, many educators remained silent. Fourth, life-adjustment education did not convey a message that students would learn basic concepts of mathematics, science, technology, and other disciplines. Progressive educators introduced the term *life adjustment* to describe programs for secondary schools that built on the "important needs of youth" expressed in the Educational Policies Commission's report *Education for All American Youth* (1944). Life-adjustment education focused on the needs of students in "general tracks" and proposed a curriculum of functional experiences in areas such as the practical arts (later to become technology education), family living, and civic participation. Such rhetoric about the curriculum seemed to neglect aspects of the disciplines that critics considered vital. Finally, progressive educators lacked (or probably never developed) public support for their ideas, while the critics' opinions had a natural appeal to the public's perceptions of what constitutes a good education. This is probably explained by the critics' appeal to basic themes such as restoration of learning, which implied students were not learning anything, especially the basics. The critics' ideas and recommendations were aligned with the educational experiences the general public had when they were in school and represented activities parents knew and could do with their children.

THE 1957 SPUTNIK MOMENT

In fall 1957, the debate about American education reached a turning point. Sputnik helped resolve the debate in favor of those who recommended greater emphasis on higher academic standards, especially in science and mathematics. Sputnik made clear to the American public that it was in the national interest to change education, in particular the curriculum for mathematics and science. Although the public had previously opposed federal aid to schools—on the grounds that federal aid would lead to federal control—a major change in American education was required. After Sputnik, the public demand for a federal response was unusually high, and Congress passed the National Defense Education Act (NDEA) in 1958. NDEA provided more on federal funding for defense-oriented personnel and student loans.

A Shared Vision

Another important point to note is that curriculum reformers of the Sputnik era shared a common vision. Across disciplines and within the education community, reformers generated enthusiasm for their initiatives. In their vision, they would replace the current content of topics and information with a curriculum based on conceptually fundamental ideas and the modes of scientific inquiry and mathematical problem solving. The reform would replace textbooks with instructional materials that included films, laboratory activities, and readings. No longer would schools' science and mathematics programs emphasize information, terms, and applied aspects of content; rather, students would learn the conceptual fundamentals and research procedures of science and mathematics disciplines.

THE FEDERAL ROLE IN EDUCATION REFORM

The reformers' vision of replacing the curriculum, combined with united political and economic support for education improvement, stimulated the reform. The Eisenhower administration (1953–1961) provided initial economic support, and the enthusiasm of the Kennedy administration (1961–1963) moved the nation forward on reform initiatives. While the Soviet Union had provided Sputnik as a symbol for the problem, President Kennedy provided a vision of a manned flight to the Moon as America's solution to the problem.

The President Clarifies a National Vision

Americans were embarrassed by the Union of Soviet Socialist Republics's (USSR) success. President Kennedy summoned Congress—and, by extension, all Americans—when he stated to a joint session of Congress on May 25, 1961:

> First, I believe that this nation should commit itself to achieving the goal, before this decade is out, of landing a man on the Moon and returning him safely to the Earth. No single space project in this period will be more impressive to mankind, or more important for the long-range exploration of space; and none will be so difficult or expensive to accomplish.

In this challenge to Congress and American citizens, the president also noted the following:

> Now it is time to take longer strides—time for a great new American enterprise—time for this nation to take a clearly leading role in space achievement, which in many ways may hold the key to our future on Earth.

> … Let it be clear that I am asking the Congress and the country to accept a firm commitment to a new course of action—a course which will last for many years and carry very heavy costs. (Kennedy 1961)

The challenge was given, and part of the response was a reform of the STEM disciplines. To be clear, it mostly was a reform of science and mathematics. The response also included a space program with a series of steps to the Moon—*Mercury*, *Gemini*, and finally *Apollo*.

I shall return to the specific discussion and vision expressed by President Kennedy, as they contain insights about what constituted the original Sputnik moment. These insights may be seen as lessons in the contemporary STEM era.

SPUTNIK AND A NATIONAL MISSION

Does the United States need another Sputnik? Clearly, there will not be another Sputnik, but we need what Sputnik has come to symbolize: a national mission and an era of significant reform of STEM education. One can identify similar concerns about national security, economic productivity, environmental quality, resource use, and health, as well as the need for scientists, engineers, and scientifically literate citizens. These issues and others present an opportunity to pause and reflect on the national mission of the Sputnik period and identify insights into our contemporary era.

Insights Concerning Reform

Here are several insights about the Sputnik era and a national mission for education. The competitor and venue were clear: the Soviet Union and a race to space (see Table 2.1). President Kennedy challenged the nation to respond by setting a clear goal: Send a man to the Moon and return him safely. The president also set a timeline: by the end of the decade. This goal had a clear and visible symbol that every American could see on a regular basis—the Moon. Accomplishing the ultimate goal included approximations of success that the public could see and understand—suborbital flights, orbital flights, a flight around the Moon and back, and ultimately landing men on the Moon and returning them safely to Earth. One component of the U.S. response involved curriculum reform led by the scientific and mathematics communities.

One final insight centers on the use of curriculum materials and science teacher institutes as primary methods of education reform. Both of these programs address the core of teachers' effective interaction with students. This was a positive and productive way the federal government used programs to facilitate educational reform.

Table 2.1. Sputnik Era and a National Mission

Goal	Send a man to the Moon and return him safely
Competitor	Union of Soviet Socialist Republics (USSR)
Metaphor	Space race
Timeline	By the end of this decade (i.e., 1969)
Symbol	The Moon
Legislation	National Defense Education Act (NDEA)
Acronyms	Used to identify curriculum projects (e.g., PSSC, BSCS, SCIS, ECCP)
Educational approach to change	Curriculum programs and professional development for teachers
STEM disciplines	Primarily science and mathematics
Leaders of education reform	Scientists and mathematicians

Who Led the Sputnik Reform?

Reformers enjoyed financial support from both public and private sources for their curriculum projects. Federal agencies, particularly the National Science Foundation (NSF), and major philanthropic foundations, particularly the Carnegie Corporation of New York and the Rockefeller Brothers Fund, provided ample support for the development of new programs.

The reformers themselves represented senior scholars from prestigious institutions such as the National Academy of Sciences (NAS), the National Academy of Engineering (NAE), and the American Mathematical Society (AMS). They had affiliations with Harvard, Massachusetts

Institute of Technology, Stanford, University of Illinois, University of Maryland, and the University of California system. In the public's and funders' views, the scientists and mathematicians who led projects during this era gave credibility and confidence that we could really achieve a revolution in American education. As Frances Keppel, then U.S. Commissioner of Education, said in 1963, "More time, talent, and money than ever before in history have been invested in pushing outward the frontiers of educational knowledge, and in the next decade or two we may expect even more significant developments" (Gross and Murphy 1964, p. 1). Keppel may have been correct about the investment and the frontiers of educational knowledge, but in the next decade, education witnessed significant developments that changed Keppel's optimistic projection of what became described as the Sputnik-based revolution in American education.

A Change in the Social and Political Climate

Americans developed a new social and political awareness as a result of the events in the 1950s. A social awareness of civil rights developed, and the origins of this awareness included the Supreme Court decision *Brown vs. Board of Education* and Governor Orval Faubus and his refusal to allow African American students to enter Little Rock Central High School. In the early 1960s, society increased its attention to civil rights, poverty, and an escalating war in Vietnam. Socially, we entered an era of criticism and protest that education did not escape. The titles of books from this period clearly express the educational protest: *Compulsory Mis-Education* (Goodman 1964), *Death at an Early Age* (Kozol 1967), *Our Children Are Dying* (Hentoff 1966), and *How Children Fail* (Holt 1964). The criticisms of this period were many, deep, wide, and continuous. At the same time, constructive solutions were few, shallow, narrow, and short-lived. Interestingly, there was a call for relevance of school programs—a call that echoed progressive ideas, although most critics did not identify them as such. Programs from the Sputnik era were included in the critics' view of what was wrong in American schools. Indeed, as the new PSSC, CBA, CHEM study, BSCS, SCIS, ESS, and other programs were reaching students, criticisms mounted regarding their elitism, the lack of relevancy, and a lack of accommodation for the diverse range of students in schools.

Just as social and political factors had initiated and supported the Sputnik era of education reform, social and political factors also arose in the 1960s and 1970s and acted as countervailing forces to the pursuits of excellence, high academic standards, and an understanding of the conceptual and methodological basis of the science, technology, engineering, and mathematics disciplines. I should also note that in the Sputnik era, political, social, and economic support—combined with the enthusiasm of scholars and a single focus on replacing curriculum programs—omitted what I consider a necessary aspect of education reform: establishing policies at the state and local levels that would sustain the innovative programs of the Sputnik era in the school system.

EDUCATION REFORM IN THE SPUTNIK ERA

First, and very important, education reform in the Sputnik era was not a failure. Education reform efforts contribute to the overall development and continuous improvement of the education system. The education community and the public learned from the experience. It also is the case that many hold the misconception that a particular reform will fix our education problems once and for all. Although the reformers made mistakes and the programs had weaknesses, the approaches the reformers used, the groups they formed, and the programs they developed have all had a positive and lasting influence on American education.

Science Curricula

Reports in the late 1970s indicated that the curriculum programs had a broad impact. The new programs were being used extensively, and commercial textbooks had incorporated innovative approaches (Weiss 1978; Helgeson, Blosser, and Howe 1977). For example, in the academic year 1976–1977, nearly 60% of school districts were using one or more of the federally funded programs in grades 7 through 12, and 30% of school districts reported using at least one program in elementary schools. Reviews of the effect of science curricula on student performance indicated that the programs were successful (i.e., student achievement was higher in Sputnik-era programs than in programs with traditional curricula), especially the BSCS programs (Shymansky, Kyle, and Alport 1983).

Technology and Engineering Curricula

ECCP began rather late in this period and was not released until 1971. For multiple reasons, it was not widely implemented.

Mathematics Curricula

Mathematics presented a different situation. Mathematicians criticized the new programs because the content was too abstract and neglected significant applications, teachers criticized the programs because they were too difficult to teach, and parents criticized the new math because they did not understand it and worried that their children would not develop fundamental computational skills. Although 30% of districts reported using NSF-supported mathematics programs in the early 1970s, only 9% reported using NSF programs in 1976–1977. Most important, mathematics teachers supported this change from Sputnik-era programs back to basic programs.

Curriculum Development Groups

Another significant but unrecognized outcome of Sputnik era was the birth of education groups that specialized in the development of instructional materials. Some of the groups continue today, such as BSCS, Lawrence Hall of Science (LHS), and Education Development Center (EDC). Furthermore, new groups that serve a similar educational function have emerged since the Sputnik era, such as the National Science Resources Center (NSRC), the Concord Consortium, and the Technical Education Resource Center (TERC).

An Influence on Future Citizens and Scientists

The Sputnik era had other indirect but important effects on the individuals and the education system. Over my years in science education, especially while working at BSCS, I have had numerous individuals talk about the influence that a particular science program, such as the BSCS Green Version, had on their lives and careers. Some of these individuals are now scientists, science educators, or science teachers, but many are not—they are citizens who have an interest in science, which is an important goal of STEM education.

Innovations in Instructional Activities

Among the significant influences from the Sputnik era are the many classroom activities and lessons that have been infused into science and mathematics education. For example, the ESS program produced activities such as "Batteries and Bulbs" and "Mystery Powders." To this day, these activities and many others are used in classrooms, undergraduate teacher education programs, and professional development workshops. Though these activities are not as nationally prominent as student achievement scores, we did effect some changes in the teaching and learning of science and mathematics.

Collaboration on Curriculum Development

I think it is quite significant that senior scientists, mathematicians, and engineers worked along with teachers and other educators on this reform. They set a precedent for current and future reforms of education. It also is significant that many educators—for example, those responsible for teacher education—were not directly involved in the reform and were slow to support it, doing so through revision of programs for certification and licensure, professional workshops for teachers, and undergraduate courses for future teachers.

The End of an Era

The Sputnik era continued into the early 1970s; if I had to indicate an end of the era, it would be 1976. *Man-A Course of Study* (MACOS), an anthropology program developed with NSF funds, came under scrutiny and widespread attack from conservative critics who objected to the subject matter (Dow 1991). The combined forces of House subcommittee hearings, NSF internal review, and the Government Accountability Office (GAO) investigation of the financial relationships between NSF and the developers signaled the end of the MACOS program and symbolized the end of an era of curriculum reform.

REFLECTIONS FROM THE SPUTNIK ERA

Although the task of education reform is complicated by the scale of the problem and complexity of the education system, the work is essential. Those interested in reform may benefit from a brief reflection on this one period in our history. Although I have stated variations of these lessons in other contexts (Bybee 1993; 1997b; 2010), I state them again not because they are new, but because the generation of STEM reform and reformers is new.

I used the noun *reflection* because it presents an interesting metaphor for an examination of the Sputnik era. Reflection suggests two things: It implies seeing something from a different angle, as in light reflected from a mirror, and also means concentration or careful consideration, as in personal reflection on past events. Reflecting on education reform, then, may mean pausing and considering an era such as Sputnik from a different angle. Most reflect on the Sputnik era and extol the zeitgeist that permeated the period and ask questions about the characteristics of different programs and whether we were successful or not. In this reflection, I am taking another approach and asking different questions. This discussion reports more than a series of observations; it is a synthesis of ideas from authors who have examined the recent history of American education, especially in science and mathematics. The discussion centers on factors that distinguish the process of education reform rather than a description of the actual content or products of a particular reform. I asked these questions: What characterizes the end of one era and the beginning of another era of education reform? What insights can we gain from those interested in reforming STEM education?

Education Reform Is Influenced by the Dominant Social and Political Vision.

Whether pursing excellence or advocating equity, conservative or liberal, progressive or traditional, the education system is subject to the dominant political views of the time. The early 1950s was a conservative period characterized by the Cold War, McCarthyism, and critics such as Hyman Rickover and Arthur Bestor, who carried conservative views to the education community. Developing science and mathematics programs with a clear emphasis on academics and discipline-based concepts and processes was consistent with the conservative social and political views. The programs were designed to nurture excellence in students and motivate them toward careers in science and engineering. Here, excellence was emphasized more than equality.

In the 1960s, there emerged the counterpoint of the Sputnik era. At that time, we witnessed a period of liberal protest that individuals such as John Holt, Paul Goodman, Nat Hentoff, Jonathan Kozol, and Herb Kohl directed toward schools. One of the dominant themes of the period was a greater emphasis on equality. There was a criticism leveled at the Sputnik-era programs that they did not appropriately address issues of equality. Although individuals criticized the new science and mathematics programs, they were still implemented in schools and used into the 1970s and beyond.

Education Reforms Eventually Have Opponents.

Regardless of the reform, a time comes when critics emerge to find fault with various ideas, policies, programs, and practices associated with the reform. Ironically, the more fundamental a reform is to education, the more criticism it will receive. The proposals for national tests receive more criticism than schemes for site-based management. It matters little what the orientation of the reform—conservative or liberal, excellence or equity, policy or program—as notable individuals will find something to criticize.

In recent decades, we have witnessed criticism for numerous, disparate, and single-issue groups. To accommodate those varied concerns, major education initiatives often attempt to incorporate diverse orientations, which are sometimes contradictory and never adequately accommodate the unique demands of different groups. In many respects, attempts at education reform become a catch-22. If you develop programs to nurture future scientists and engineers, such as those in the Sputnik era, you are subject to protest from those who champion equity for the disadvantaged, as happened in the 1960s. Ironically, if you propose that policies and programs should accommodate *all* students—such as national standards for science and mathematics in the 1990s, Common Core Standards, and the Next Generation Science Standards—you are criticized by both factions, each claiming you omit the unique needs of their constituent students.

In STEM education, we lack unity and agreement on our purposes. Although I have stated a purpose in Chapter 1, one has concern about its acceptance. When individuals or groups try to state such goals through national standards, for example, those too are subject to criticism from both the left and the right. The education system is more chaotic than coherent, and at best it represents a loosely connected set of components that act without systems for coordination, regulation, and defense against those factors that can harm the system.

Education Critics Distort the Ideas of Reform Initiatives.

The distorted views seen in contemporary reform are not a new phenomenon. Arthur Bestor, one of the most powerful critics of progressive education, presented his opinions with little evidence, and some were clearly erroneous. For example, Bestor (1953) asked, "Why is there no reference to arithmetic in the Educational Policies Commission report *Education for All American Youth?*" Yet arithmetic was discussed in the context of college preparation, vocational training, and elective programs. Likewise, liberal critics of the 1960s were subject to the distortions, overstatement, and lack of evidence to support their positions.

In this era of standards-based reform, contemporary critics continue to equate voluntary national standards with federal mandates and policy documents with education programs that by most reports only marginally represent standards. They criticize what goes on in classrooms, claiming it is based on standards, when the evidence indicates that the influence of standards on classroom teaching is not widespread.

Education Reforms Distort the Costs, Risks, and Benefits of New Initiatives.

Even the curriculum reformers of the Sputnik era tended to distort their claims of how the education system would change as a result of the new programs. It would seem that any call for education revolution is ill advised. Mostly revolutionary perspectives represent powerful rhetoric and a poor understanding of the relative change in education systems.

Education Systems Incorporate the Language of Reform.

Educators quickly begin using some reform ideas, and they are especially ready to adopt language and terminology associated with the reform. STEM is a contemporary example. Educators have the language but lack the deeper conceptual understanding of the ideas. In the Progressive Era, most educators talked about child-centered classrooms and experience-based programs, but seldom did they change their teaching strategies. In the Sputnik era, we talked of inquiry but seldom implemented it in practice. As a recent example, most state and many local school districts have incorporated the language of standards, especially of the *National Science Education Standards* (NRC 1996) or *Benchmarks for Science Literacy* (AAAS 1993) into frameworks. However, they failed to view the documents as total statements, omitting standards and adding new topics (as opposed to standards). They often do not include the history and nature of science and add topics such as marine biology or environmental science, which are course titles rather than standards.

Other examples include the claims by commercial publishers that their products are aligned with the orientation of the current reform. For example, textbooks are advertised as aligning with mathematics and science standards. The use of STEM to describe a variety of products is now significant.

Education Reforms Place Extraordinary Demands on Teachers.

Whether it is John Dewey's child-centered programs, the Sputnik era's inquiry-oriented curriculum, the open classrooms of the 1960s, or contemporary standards-based movements, the demands on teachers' time and abilities were unreasonable. In most cases, the reformers clearly underestimated the teachers' resistance to reform; reluctance to discard old practices; and hesitance to change their beliefs, attitudes, and values about teaching.

Closely related to extraordinary demands is the lack of resources in the support of classroom teachers. During the Progressive Era, teachers were asked to develop curriculum without the administration's support; in the Sputnik era, they were asked to implement new curriculum without school-based support; now they are held accountable for having all students meet high standards without provision programs, professional development, or systemic support. Although I think all components of education systems need to engage in continuous development—and this includes teachers—given the demands and lack of support, for teachers not to respond seems to be a rational response.

In the Sputnik era, teachers said it early and often: If I teach by inquiry, I will not cover the subject. Joseph Schwab's (1966; 1978a; 1978b; 1978c) and Jerome Bruner's (1960) poignant discussions and insightful arguments for inquiry did not persuade the teachers to change. Reformers who present policies and develop new programs must realize the fundamental importance and difficulty of basic changes in teachers' practices.

Education Reformers Have Failed to Educate the Public About Reform.

We have tended to convert educators and ignore the public's education about the ideas we propose. Time and again, reforms did not have public support, and reform ideas easily succumbed to widespread criticism and often misrepresentation of what the reform was all about.

A clear indicator of the reformers' failure to educate the public about new initiatives is the cry to return to an education that the public experienced, or that a mathematics program that has real-world problems somehow ignores basic mathematical skills. Insights from contemporary research on learning should help us understand that the public's prior experience and knowledge dominates the conception of education. Reformers should consider how conceptual change models of learning would apply to the public's education about innovative programs and practices. In many respects, the current debates about standards, in particular mathematics, easily convert the public because there is little or no initial education and subsequent understanding about the new ideas and approaches. Once the criticism begins, it is difficult to counter the positions put forward by critics.

Education Reformers Often Criticize More Than They Construct.

Few individuals, agencies, or organizations expend time and energy trying to provide new models. It is easier to criticize than to engage in the steady work of establishing new policies, programs, or practices. The latter requires more time, support, and endurance of the inevitable criticism. This said, the long-term contribution to American education lies in the positive contributions of those who build more than they destroy.

Education Reformers Often Fail to Address the Problem of Scale.

In the Sputnik era, reformers assumed their programs would get to scale simply if they place the programs in the education system. They were wrong. It is clear that one cannot introduce something at the national level—be it standards, curriculum, or a test—and expect it to take hold locally. You cannot simply point to exemplary programs or best practices and assume they will spread throughout the education system like a viral infection. The infectious disease metaphor indicated why this assumption usually fails: The education system has an extremely powerful immune system with antibodies that quickly neutralize, inhibit the growth, and destroy innovations.

Education Reformers Have Not Learned From the Past.

This lesson is my reason for including this chapter. Education lacks a long-term memory. We do not recall, for example, what went right or wrong with progressive education or the Sputnik-spurred programs. We do not realize that a reform is connected to social and political times, and those will change. We ignore teachers' needs, even when they tell us what they need. We lack the insight to educate the public, then lament the poor understanding of new ideas and critics' misrepresentation of education initiatives.

CONCLUSION

Amid the contemporary use of Sputnik as a signal of the need for education reform, it may be important to answer the question, "What can we learn from the original Sputnik moment?" Among the answers to this question that may have implications for the STEM era, I would note the following: The reform initiative centered on development of curriculum materials; this was a constructive role of the federal government; the national mission was clear and widely supported; for the most part the reforms were led by the scientific community; and the beginning and end of the Sputnik era were clearly influenced by political, social, and cultural forces.

Several other lessons may apply to contemporary education reform. Among the important lessons from the original Sputnik era, I would point to the aforementioned social and political influences; the role of critics; the distortion of costs, benefits, and risks by both critics and advocates; the failure to educate the public about the reasons for and advantages of the reform; and, finally, the extraordinary demands placed on teachers who have to implement the changes in programs and practices.

DISCUSSION QUESTIONS

1. How would you describe the beginning, middle, and end of the original Sputnik moment?

2. What lessons would you synthesize from the original Sputnik reform, and how would you apply those lessons to contemporary education reform?

3. Assuming the importance of a national mission as integral as a Sputnik moment, what would you argue is (or should be) the contemporary national vision?

4. What role might critics play in the creation, development, and demise of STEM education?

CHAPTER 3

Is STEM Education a Response to This Generation's Sputnik Moment?

H ere is my answer to the question that leads this chapter: If this is a Sputnik moment, then yes, STEM education should be part of a response. However, the total burden of the nation's response should not be placed on education. That has been tried before, and it doesn't work very well for either the nation or education. This chapter assumes a positive answer to the earlier question and proceeds to clarify what the response might entail. To begin, I will review the features of a Sputnik moment. I will then place STEM responses in the context of several additional lessons from the Sputnik era.

IS THIS A SPUTNIK MOMENT?

Chapter 2 reviewed the Sputnik era and included a table that summarized a number of features that characterized the era. Table 3.1 (p. 26) includes the summary from Chapter 2 and suggests features for the present era. President John F. Kennedy's speech to a joint session of Congress on May 25, 1961, has themes that are as appropriate today as they were then:

> We intend to be first. In short, our leadership in science and industry, our hopes
> for peace and security, our obligations to ourselves as well as others, all require
> us to make this effort, to solve these mysteries, to solve them for the good of all
> men, and to become the world's leading space-faring nation. (Kennedy 1961)

Before I begin a discussion of specific action for STEM education, it seems appropriate to cover a few additional lessons from the first Sputnik moment. I have revised and restated these from *The Teaching of Science: 21st-Century Perspectives* (Bybee 2010). There are calls for "a commitment to innovation" and a need to "win the future" by leaders of business, the scientific and engineering community, and policy makers. In the context of a "Sputnik moment," I would rate that the innovation that initiated the original Sputnik moment was a need to get a man to the Moon. The challenge was large and the goal specific and understandable to all concerned. Although we do need to attend to poor levels of achievement on national and international assessments, these issues are not major events perpetrated by external competitors (i.e., Sputnik moments). Examples of new and major innovations have been suggested by President Barack Obama to address energy efficiency and the use of national resources, improved health care, economic stability, and stronger national security, among other areas.

Innovations in these and other areas will have positive and long-term effects on the United States. The path to innovations in these areas certainly could be related to STEM education, better training for the workforce, and support for research and development.

Table 3.1. Features of a Sputnik Moment—Past and Present

Features of a Sputnik Moment	1960s	2012 and beyond
Goal	Send a man to the Moon and return him safely	Become a world leader in innovation
Competitor	USSR	Economic competitors (e.g., India, China)
Metaphor	Space race	Economic progress
Timeline	Decade	2 decades
Symbol	Moon	Stock market
Legislation	National Defense Education Act (NDEA)	Reauthorization of Elementary & Secondary Education Act (ESEA; also known as No Child Left Behind)
Acronyms	Used to identify programs (e.g., BSCS, PSSC, SCIS, ECCP)	STEM used as a slogan for one aspect of education reform
Educational approach to change	Curriculum reform	"Race to the Top" projects, national standards, and aligned assessments
STEM disciplines	Primarily science and math	All STEM disciplines
Leaders of education reform	Scientists and mathematicians	Educators at the state, district, and school levels

IF THIS IS A SPUTNIK MOMENT, HERE ARE MORE LESSONS TO CONSIDER.

The Sputnik era reveals some insights worth noting for those interested in reforms related to STEM education. I will now present several more lessons from the Sputnik era.

Replacing Traditional Discipline-Based Programs Is Extremely Difficult at Best.

Although leaders in the Sputnik era used terms such as *revision* and *reform*, the intention was to totally replace school science and mathematics programs. The leaders' zeal and confidence were great. In some sense, they approached the reform as a field of dreams. That is, the leaders believed that if they built excellent curriculum materials, then teachers would adopt them, thus replacing traditional programs. Such an approach, however, confronts pervasive institutional resistance, raises the personal concerns of teachers, and alarms the public. The need to understand what happened in the Sputnik era contributed to research on curriculum implementation, concerns of teachers, and changes in education.

Relative to curriculum-based STEM initiatives, one lesson centers on the importance of using our knowledge about education change (Hall and Hord 1987; 2001; Fullan 2001). Not only would new STEM programs be important, but other components of the education system must also change and provide support for the implementation of STEM-based innovations. Those components include peer teachers; school administrators; school boards; the community; and a variety of local, state, and national policies.

There is a second related lesson: Do not try to replace the entire constellation of traditional programs. Approaching STEM education as though it (whatever *it* is) will be a revolution and totally replace science disciplines and mathematics courses is unlikely and unreasonable. I propose an evolutionary perspective, one that uses short curriculum units and incremental change and slowly establishes an environment that continually selects for the education innovations—STEM.

Resistance to Reform Is Proportional to the Degree to Which the Innovations Vary From Current Programs and Practices: The Greater the Change, the More Resistance.

Teachers had difficulty with the content and pedagogy of new programs from the Physical Science Study Committee (PSSC), Biological Sciences Curriculum Study (BSCS), Chemical Bond Approach (CBA), Chemical Education Materials Study (CHEM Study), Earth Science Curriculum Project (ESCP), Science Curriculum Improvement Study (SCIS), Engineering Concepts Curriculum Project (ECCP), and Elementary Science Study (ESS). Lacking support within their local systems and experiencing political criticism from outside education, teachers sought security by staying with or returning to the traditional programs.

The lesson here centers on several things: the importance of both initial and ongoing professional development; administrative support for new programs; the need for education reformers to recognize that changes in social and political forces have an effect on school programs; and, finally, a need for awareness of how much the STEM innovations vary from current programs.

Excluding Groups Can Result in Difficulties, Especially for Critical Components of the Education System.

During the Sputnik era, many in the larger science and mathematics education communities (e.g., teacher educators, science education researchers, and the public) contributed to the slow acceptance and implementation of the new programs, reduced understanding by those entering the profession, and initially afforded less-than-adequate professional development for teachers in the classroom. The reason for the slow acceptance and implementation now seems clear: Many in the science and mathematics education communities were not included in reform initiatives until late in the effort.

This lesson was clearly a case for the involvement of technology and engineering. Early in the Sputnik era, the scientists made every effort to exclude technology and engineering from their respective curriculum programs. See, for example, discussions about engineering in *Scientists in the Classroom* (Rudolph 2002, p. 116).

Those interested in STEM initiatives must involve more than teachers. Education is a system consisting of many different components. One important component consists of those who have some responsibility for state standards and assessments, state certifications, teacher preparation, professional development, and the potential implementation of STEM programs at the school level. It is best to work from a perspective that attempts to unify and coordinate efforts among teachers, administrators, teacher educators, scientists, engineers, technologists, and mathematicians, all of whom have strengths and weaknesses in their respective contributions to various STEM initiatives.

State and Local Priorities and Policies Must Be Recognized.

In the Sputnik era, support from federal agencies and national foundations freed developers from the political and educational constraints of state and local agencies and the power and influence of commercial publishers.

This lesson directs those interested in STEM to a broader, more systemic view of education, one that includes a variety of policies. My view of education involves purposes, policies, programs, and practices (i.e., the 4Ps, which were discussed in Chapter 1). Individuals, organizations, and agencies usually contribute in various ways to establishing purposes in the formulating of policies, developing programs, or implementing practices; however, there must be coordination and consistency among the various efforts. Designing and developing new programs, such as we did in the Sputnik era, without attending to a larger education context to support those programs and changing classroom practices to align with the innovative program surely will minimize the success of the initiative.

Restricting Initiatives to Specific Groups Results in Criticisms.

To the degree to which school systems implemented the new programs, teachers found that the materials were inappropriate for some populations of students and too difficult for others. Restricting policies or targeting programs opens the door to criticism that centers on equity. Proposing initiatives for *all* students also often results in criticism from both those who maintain there is a need for a specific program for those inclined toward science, engineering, or mathematics and those who argue that programs for all somehow discriminate against the disadvantaged.

Examining the nature and lessons of Sputnik-era reforms, as well as those that came before and after, clearly demonstrates that education reforms differ. Although this may seem obvious, policy makers and educators have not always paid attention to some of the common themes and general lessons that may benefit the steady work of improving science education. Stated succinctly, those lessons are to use what we know about education change; include all the key players in the STEM education community; align STEM education policies, programs, and practices with the stated purposes of education; work on improving STEM education for all students; and attend to the support and continuous professional development of STEM teachers because they are the most essential resource in the system of STEM education.

What Might a STEM Response Include?

No Child Left Behind (NCLB) has dominated the education landscape, and the significant features—establish high standards; develop highly qualified teachers; and test students yearly in grades 3–8 on math, reading, and science (the latter began in the 2007–2008 school year)—have directed educators' attention to teacher accountability and student achievement. Relative to this discussion, I would note the lack of attention to curriculum—in particular, instructional materials that bridge state standards and student assessments, the marginal attention to high school, the high use of negative or perverse incentives for yearly progress, and the perception that NCLB is an unfunded mandate.

A STEM response to the Sputnik moment should include a clear purpose with specific education outcomes and the means to achieve those goals. I would refer the reader to earlier discussions of purpose (i.e., the goals) and categories of education policy; curricular, instruction, and assessment programs; and classroom practices. One purpose of this book is to help individuals develop responses to these categories of change within the context of their leadership at, for example, the national, state, district, and school levels.

AFTER ALMOST A DECADE OF NCLB, WHAT HAS THE UNITED STATES ACHIEVED?

U.S. Students Are Average, and Average Is Not the Leadership We Need.

After nearly a decade of efforts to improve students' achievement, the results of 15-year-olds are presented in Table 3.2 (p. 30). U.S. students are average in reading and science and slightly below average in mathematics. These results are from the Program for International Student Assessments (PISA).

One conclusion that seems clear is that the United States continues to fall behind its economic competitors despite No Child Left Behind and a variety of reforms. The results displayed in Table 3.2 (p. 30) are cause for concern, but they do not constitute a Sputnik moment. They represent American potential to respond to this generation's Sputnik moment—if we can define it and establish a clear and compelling national mission.

Beyond the realization that students in the United States do not perform well on international assessments such as PISA, one lesson we learn from high-achieving countries—those that we generally see as economic competitors—is that they have high levels of coherence in their science and mathematics curricula. The United States must find a way to achieve greater coherence in STEM programs while still honoring states' and local jurisdictions' right to select and establish curricula. Achieving this goal requires careful attention to standards, understanding and using instructional materials that are coherent, and viewing the school program vertically (i.e., K–12) and not just horizontally (i.e., at each grade level).

There is a consistent call for individuals with higher levels of abilities such as problem solving, critical thinking, and reasoning. According to recent results on the PISA survey, American students do not perform well on problem-solving tasks (Lemke et al. 2004). They ranked 24 out of 29 on such tasks among students in participating OECD countries. Many of these are countries with which we compete economically. Within STEM, teaching science

Table 3.2. Results of 15-Year-Olds From the Top 10 Countries and the United States From PISA 2009

Rank	Country	Reading Score (OECD Average Score: 493)	Rank	Country	Math Score (OECD Average Score: 496)	Rank	Country	Science Score (OECD Average Score: 501)
1	Shanghai	556	1	Shanghai	600	1	Shanghai	575
2	South Korea	539	2	Singapore	562	2	Finland	554
3	Finland	536	3	Hong Kong	555	3	Hong Kong	549
4	Hong Kong	533	4	South Korea	546	4	Singapore	542
5	Singapore	526	5	Taiwan	543	5	Japan	539
6	Canada	524	6	Finland	541	6	South Korea	538
7	New Zealand	521	7	Liechtenstein	536	7	New Zealand	532
8	Japan	520	8	Switzerland	534	8	Canada	529
9	Australia	515	9	Japan	529	9	Estonia	528
10	Netherlands	508	10	Canada	527	10	Australia	527
17	United States	500	31	United States	487	23	United States	502

Source: OECD 2009b.

Note: The high averages for Shanghai and Hong Kong do not represent all of Chinese education. They are special administrative regions of China that participated in PISA 2009.

as inquiry and engineering as design seems a straightforward way to address the issue of enhancing problem-solving abilities. Although there seems to be a clear need for higher levels of achievement in basic science concepts, developing the abilities of scientific inquiry and engineering design would contribute to the preparation of a 21st-century workforce.

CONCLUSION

From classrooms to the highest political office, during the Sputnik era people responded in positive and constructive ways given the perceived crisis and national mission. Science curricula and support for implementation were based on teachers' interests and abilities. We answered science teachers' needs and concerns as the Sputnik era developed. Insights from that era should be considered as the nation prepares for a new reform of STEM education. There will not be another actual Sputnik satellite, but using Sputnik as a metaphor for education reform is timely. Is STEM education a response to this generation's Sputnik moments? The answer is yes.

DISCUSSION QUESTIONS

1. In your view, is STEM education a response to this generation's Sputnik moment? Explain why or why not.

2. This chapter and Chapter 2 use quotes from President John F. Kennedy. How would you explain the importance of presidential statements in education reform?

3. Based on the lessons from earlier reforms, what would you argue is an appropriate education response to this generation's Sputnik moment?

CHAPTER 4

How Is STEM Education Reform Different From Other Education Reforms?

"How is this education reform different from any other reform?" In the context of this chapter, the answer to this question is what differentiates STEM reform from other reforms, such as the Sputnik era. The answer gives some clarity to the meaning of STEM education. What makes a STEM reform different resides in four themes:

- Addressing global challenges that citizens must understand
- Changing perceptions of environmental and associated problems
- Recognizing 21st-century workforce skills
- Continuing issues of national security

Globalization has steadily increased in relevance in discussions about STEM education. Although abstract, the term *globalization* has captured our imagination and emerged as a theme with the potential for significant innovations. Because globalization is somewhat ambiguous, the term does not in and of itself suggest what those innovations might be. Indeed, most contemporary discussions of globalization variously describe processes, conditions, systems, forces, and historical eras and center on social relations, communications, economics, and politics. A discussion of the possible connections between globalization and STEM education and the identification of subsequent innovations for STEM education seem timely and appropriate.

This chapter has three parts. The first part uses global challenges to present themes that connect globalization and STEM education. Several of these themes, such as environmental problems, are understandable and easily connect to STEM education. The second section will cover other themes, such as economics, that will be unique to many in the STEM education community. The third part presents 21st-century skills and innovations implied by global challenges. The discussions in the chapter answer the question, How is the STEM reform different from other education reforms?

GLOBAL CHALLENGES FOR CITIZENS AND SOCIETIES

In considering the connections between globalization, STEM education, and the connective tissue of global challenges, one can rightfully ask an initial question: What constitutes a global challenge? A second reasonable question follows: Which problems are clearly appropriate for STEM education? Finally, what are the appropriate responses for the STEM education community?

Connecting Global Challenges and STEM Education

Answering the first question—What constitutes a global challenge?—centers on cross-border effects and issues related to the "global commons." These issues have to do with sharing the planet with others and recognizing use (and overuse) of common resources such as the atmosphere, biodiversity and ecosystem losses, deforestation, water deficits, and fisheries depletion. The consequences are problems such as global climate change, ecological scarcity, and emerging and re-emerging infectious diseases. These global challenges clearly have connections to the STEM disciplines and, subsequently, to international economics, politics, and national security (Rischard 2002).

Responding to the second question—Which problems are clearly appropriate for STEM education?—centers on the global problems for which the STEM disciplines provide insights, explanations, and potential solutions. Finally, the responses from the STEM education community require clarification of STEM literacy as an aim and the identification of new learning outcomes, curriculum programs, and teaching practices.

In education, the STEM disciplines have a long history of responding to societal issues, and we are now being called to address new challenges that extend beyond the personal and societal realms to global dimensions. Even a cursory review of daily news reports, National Research Council (NRC) reports (see, e.g., NRC 2009), or presidential addresses at the American Association for the Advancement of Science (AAAS) provides indicators for the theme of global challenges: "Reflections on Our Planet and Its Life, Origin, and Futures" (McCarthy 2009); "Science and Technology for Sustainable Well-Being" (Holdren 2008); "Grand Challenges and Great Opportunities in Science, Technology, and Public Policy" (Omenn 2006); "The Nexus: Where Science Meets Society" (Jackson 2005); and "The Grand Challenges of Engineering" (see *www.engineeringchallenges.org*) could also be added to this list. To be more specific, global challenges include topics such as climate change, health, energy efficiency, environmental quality, resources use, natural hazards, national security, and general themes of sustainable development (Sachs 2004).

Challenges for the STEM Education Community

Globally, there are myriad and unique challenges. In coming decades, nations must begin addressing STEM-related challenges that have general implications for education and the literacy of citizens. Our globe needs citizens who understand and are ready to address STEM-related challenges such as the following:

- Economic stability and the development of a 21st-century workforce
- Energy efficiency and adequate responses for a carbon-constrained world
- Environmental quality and the need for evidence-based responses to global climate change
- Resource use and the need to address continuing conflicts over limited natural resources

- Mitigation of natural hazards by preparing for severe weather, earthquakes, and fires
- Health maintenance and the need to reduce the spread of preventable diseases
- Public understanding of the role of scientific advances and technological innovations in health and human welfare

The global challenges citizens face are clearly significant and will require more than an education solution, but STEM education must be part of any response. The education response requires more than tinkering at the margins of current policies, programs, and research priorities and updating life, Earth, and physical science disciplines. The reform requires significant innovations for STEM education in general and, in my view, the curriculum in particular. The next sections explore themes that extend beyond the traditional school disciplines of science and math. Educators must rethink the fundamental content for school programs and address the 21st-century challenges.

CHANGING PERCEPTIONS OF ENVIRONMENTAL PROBLEMS

The perspective here centers on the observations that debates about, for example, global climate change have altered public perceptions about environmental problems; the role of science, technology, engineering, and mathematics in understanding and solving problems; and the connections between environmental problems and economics, politics, and societal values. Heightened environmental awareness and changed perceptions did not emerge from major reforms in traditional school science programs. Rather, the public's education likely occurred through the media, informal education, and various supplemental and ancillary programs in formal education.

Linking the Environment and Economics

Although perceptions and some attitudes about the environment have changed in recent times, major policy changes have been driven by economics, politics, and, most recently, national security. Since the 1960s, there has been a steady development of knowledge and understanding about the global environment and related problems. At first, this understanding centered on science and technology and was popularized by individuals such as Rachel Carson (1962), Paul Ehrlich (1968), and Garrett Hardin (1968) and publications such as *The Global 2000 Report to the President* (Barney 1980). These individuals and publications began introducing the social, economic, and political aspects of environmental problems. Groups such as the Natural Resources Defense Council (NRDC) and Worldwatch Institute began sending clear and consistent signals about increasing environmental problems and the counterpoint of sustainable development. My point here is this: In time, discussions of the environment have increasingly addressed global problems and incorporated aspects of all the STEM disciplines as well as social sciences, in particular economics and politics. Discourse has, for example, gone from scientific understanding of ecosystems to an understanding of ecosystem services and the implications of balancing resource conservation and use based on societies' values concerning consumptive (e.g., food and fuel) and nonconsumptive (e.g., health and aesthetics) services provided by ecosystems (Perrings et al. 2010).

Few have made more compelling cases for the link between global economics and the environment than Lester Brown in *Eco-Economy: Building an Economy for the Earth* (Brown 2001),

The Earth Policy Reader (Brown, Larsen, and Fischlowitz-Roberts 2002), and *Plan B 3.0: Mobilizing to Save Civilization* (Brown 2008). While making the point that the relationship between the global economy and the Earth's ecosystems is increasingly stressed, Brown and his colleagues succinctly review the strengths and weaknesses of our present economic perceptions:

> The market economy has brought a wealth to the world that our ancestors could not even have imagined. It allocates resources among competing uses, it balances supply and demand, and it facilitates the specialization that underpins the productivity of modern economics. But as the economy expands, the market's weaknesses are beginning to surface. Three stand out: its lack of respect for the sustainable-yield thresholds of natural systems, its inability to value nature's services properly, and its failure to incorporate the indirect costs of providing goods and services into their prices. (Brown, Larsen, and Fischlowitz-Roberts 2002, p. 31)

Although Brown and his colleagues did not mention national security in this part, any contemporary review of either the economy or the environment mandates consideration of the causes and consequences for national security and the causes and consequences of conflicts.

Adding Sustainability to Ecology and Economics

The 20th century witnessed the rise of science and technology and an increasing awareness of environmental and resource problems. The contemporary environmental movement has relied on knowledge from scientific research and implemented many technologies designed to ameliorate the diversity and scale of environmental problems. As environmental problems have developed at all levels, from local to global, we have seen science and technology addressed as both the possible causes and the potential solutions. Relative to this discussion, the STEM disciplines also have become factors in political and economic decision making. More than any other time in history, science, technology, engineering, mathematics, and the environment now have direct links to human health and the goods and services that contribute to personal and social welfare.

Out of necessity, many in the scientific and engineering communities have turned their attention to the environment, increased our understanding of environmental issues, and broadened our perspectives by, for example, making clear which services are provided by ecosystems. Unfortunately, some insights only emerge when the ecological services become disrupted and diminished.

One role of science and technology is to help us understand the physical world and the consequences of human intervention in natural systems. But science can only tell us what did or will happen, not what *should* happen. Human decisions influence the direction, rate, and scale of change. As mentioned in the previous section, many of the decisions are directed by economic motives that have detrimental environmental consequences. The concept of sustainability serves as a counterpoint to current economic perspectives (Brown 1981) and connections to STEM education (Holbrook 2009).

In *Eco-Economy: Building an Economy for the Earth* (2001), Lester Brown states the case and challenge:

> Transforming our environmentally destructive economy into one that can sustain progress depends on a Copernican shift in our economic mindset, recognition that the economy is part of Earth's ecosystem and can sustain progress only if it is restructured so that it is compatible with it. The preeminent challenge for our generation is to design an eco-economy, one that respects the principles of ecology. A redesigned economy can be integrated into the ecosystem in a way that will stabilize the relationship between the two, enabling economic progress to continue. (p. 21)

This extract that provides important insights about the enormity of the challenge and the central place of ecology. Brown continues by identifying ecological principles that would be among those considered fundamental to an education in science and the environment with a global perspective:

> Unfortunately, present-day economics does not provide the conceptual framework needed to build such an economy. It will have to be designed with an understanding of basic ecological concepts such as sustainable yield, carrying capacity, nutrient cycles, the hydrological cycle, and the climate system. Designers must also know that natural systems provide not only goods, but also services— services that are often more valuable than the goods. (Brown 2001, p. 22)

In the early years of the 21st century, the United Nations Educational, Scientific and Cultural Organization (UNESCO) designated the years 2005–2015 as a decade of education for sustainable development. This UNESCO initiative has resulted in some countries, such as Germany, teaching students about issues related to sustainable development. This discussion set the stage for STEM education and innovations inspired by a global perspective.

RECOGNIZING 21ST-CENTURY WORKFORCE SKILLS

A quote from Dr. Alan Greenspan's testimony to the U.S. Congressional Committee on Education and the Workforce in September 2000 sets several themes for this section:

> [I]n today's economy, it is becoming evident that a significant upgrading or activation of underutilized intellectual skills will be necessary to effectively engage the newer technologies. (Greenspan 2000, p. 2)

Greenspan identifies several important points. He provides an economic justification for reform of STEM education and highlights "intellectual skills," which are later discussed as 21st-century workforce skills aligned with scientific inquiry and engineering design (Bybee 2010). He clearly emphasizes technology—an implicit goal of education that should be explicit and a priority in the theme of globalization and STEM education.

Changing Demands for Intellectual Skills

Just more than a century ago, many nations faced a period of substantial social change. The industrial revolution presented new demands on the intellectual skills of workers; they had to develop the cognitive skills to operate equipment in factories, manage production lines, and direct emerging transportation and communications systems. In that era, the equivalent of a high school education became a requirement for workers in many countries.

The 20th century was a period of significant scientific advances and technological innovations, both of which contributed to dramatic social progress. As a nation's economy advanced, the requirements for skilled workers increased, especially the need for intellectual skills, including those often associated with science, technology, engineering, and mathematics.

By 21st-century standards, the intellectual skills required in the early 20th century were low. With time, nations realized the economic value of creative ideas and efficient means for the production and delivery of goods and services. As the 20th century progressed, the number of individuals in jobs requiring manual labor and routine cognitive skills steadily decreased, while the number of jobs that required intellectual abilities and the ability to solve nonroutine problems increased. In short, work became more analytical and technical. During the past century, entry-level requirements for the workforce increased to levels beyond a high school education. Taking this general observation to the more specific, one would have to note the combined role of science, technology, engineering, and mathematics as a driving force of economic change and the steady shift in requirements for entry into the workforce, especially in developed countries. The changes just described suggest a fundamental place for science, technology, engineering, and mathematics in our economy and, by extension, in our education programs. The next section addresses the connections between 21st-century skills and STEM education.

21st-Century Workforce Skills

In 2007, the National Academies held workshops that identified five broad skills that accommodated a range of jobs, from low-skill, low-wage service to high-wage, high-skill professional work. Individuals can develop these broad skills in STEM classrooms and programs, as well as in other settings (NRC 2008; 2010; Levy and Murnane 2004).

Research indicates that individuals learn and apply broad 21st-century skills within the context of specific bodies of knowledge (NRC 2008; 2010; Levy and Murnane 2004). At work, development of these skills is intertwined with development of technical content knowledge. Similarly, in STEM education, students may develop cognitive skills while engaged in the study of specific STEM-related social or global situations. The following discussion presents five skill sets important for the 21st century. Those skill sets include adaptability, complex communications, nonroutine problem solving, self-management, and systems thinking. These skills are summarized from the NRC report *Exploring the Intersection of Science Education and 21st-Century Skills* (2010).

Adaptability includes the ability and willingness to cope with uncertain, new, and rapidly changing conditions on the job, including responding effectively to emergencies or crisis situations and learning new tasks, technologies, and procedures. Adaptability also includes handling work stress; adapting to different personalities, communication styles, and cultures; and adapting physically to various indoor or outdoor work environments (Houston 2007; Pulakos, Arad, Donnovan, and Plamondon 2000).

Complex communications and social skills include skills in processing and interpreting both verbal and nonverbal information from others in order to respond appropriately. A skilled communicator selects key pieces of a complex idea to express in words, sounds, and images as a way to build shared understanding (Levy and Murnane 2004). Skilled communicators negotiate positive outcomes with customers, subordinates, and superiors through social perceptiveness, persuasion, negotiation, instructing, and service orientation (Peterson et al. 1999).

Nonroutine problem-solving skills include a skilled individual using expert thinking to examine a broad span of information, recognizing patterns, and narrowing the information to diagnose a problem. Moving beyond diagnosis to a solution requires knowledge of how the information is linked conceptually and involves metacognition—the ability to reflect on whether a problem-solving strategy is working and to switch to another strategy if the current strategy is not working (Levy and Murnane 2004). Nonroutine problem solving includes creating new and innovative solutions, integrating seemingly unrelated information, and entertaining possibilities (Houston 2007).

Self-management and self-development include personal skills needed to work remotely, in virtual teams; to work autonomously; and to be self-motivating and self-monitoring. One aspect of self-management is the willingness and ability to acquire new information and skills related to work (Houston 2007).

Systems thinking includes understanding how an entire system works; recognizing how an action, change, or malfunction in one part of the system affects other components of the system; and adopting a "big picture" perspective on work (Houston 2007). It includes decision making, systems analysis, and systems evaluation, as well as abstract reasoning about how the different elements of a work process interact (Peterson et al. 1999; Meadows 2008).

The NRC recently published another more detailed report, *Education for Life and Work: Developing Transferable Knowledge and Skills in the 21st Century* (NRC 2012). These 21st-century skills reveal a mixture of cognitive abilities, social skills, personal motivation, conceptual knowledge, and problem-solving competencies. Although a diverse group of skills, this knowledge and many of these skills and abilities can be developed in STEM programs that include scientific inquiry, technological innovation, and mathematical computation. That said, it should be made clear that STEM education cannot, and probably should not, assume sole and exclusive responsibility for developing 21st-century skills.

THE ISSUE OF NATIONAL SECURITY

Until September 11, 2001, an economic perspective would have been justification enough for education reform with a much greater recognition of STEM education. The tragic events on that date added national security to the rationale for education reform. A major point from *Road Map for National Security: Imperative for Change* (United States Commission on National Security/21st Century 2001) is worth noting. After terrorism, the greatest threat to national security (according to this report) resides in our research and education. The Commission's report stated the following:

> In this Commission's view, the inadequacies of our systems of research and education pose a greater threat to U.S. national security over the next quarter century than any potential conventional war that we might imagine. American national leadership must understand these deficiencies as threats to national security. If we do not invest heavily and wisely in rebuilding these two core strengths, America will be incapable of maintaining its global position long into the 21st century. (p. IX)

In the period immediately following September 11, several of the recommendations from this report were implemented. Now is the time to address the importance of education, because the current inadequacies—such as low levels of achievement on international assessments—certainly leave the nation in a vulnerable position.

CONCLUSION

STEM reform differs from other education reforms in four major ways. There is a need to address global challenges citizens face, recognize changing perceptions of problems related to the environment, and address the requirements for a 21st-century workforce. Finally, the issue of national security has emerged as a new and unique concern.

DISCUSSION QUESTIONS

1. How is contemporary reform of STEM education different from other education reforms?

2. Are 21st-century skills different from traditional skills and abilities developed by education in the STEM disciplines?

3. Would you add a theme to those discussed in this chapter? If so, what is the theme, and how do you justify its addition?

CHAPTER 5

STEM Education Seems to Be the Answer— What Was the Question?

In a May 2011 editorial for *NSTA Reports*, Secretary of Education Arne Duncan stated:

> Frequently when I talk with teachers, they ask, "Why is the department so focused on the STEM subjects: science, technology, engineering, and mathematics?" I tell them that the world is changing and that scientific knowledge and skills are essential for success in the knowledge economy.

Here, the question seems to have been, What do we need to develop a knowledge economy? The answer: Focus on the STEM subjects—science, technology, engineering, and mathematics. In this chapter, I direct attention to 35 reports and publications that address STEM education and identify the justification for a focus on STEM. Secretary Duncan provides one reason: We need STEM subjects for success in a knowledge economy. As you read the summaries in this chapter, try to note other justifications, such as improved student learning, job demands, international competitiveness, and a society that can respond to contemporary STEM-related issues.

I have not reviewed all the contemporary reports providing perspectives on education reform and STEM. There are too many. In 2006 and 2007, the Biological Sciences Curriculum Study (BSCS) had funding from the Office of Science Education of the National Institutes of Health (NIH) to conduct a review and synthesis of 20 reports. A summary of that publication immediately follows this introduction. After that, I provide a summary of 15 other reports and articles. In each case, I paraphrase the report's title as a question and try to indicate how STEM education might be an answer to the question.

THE BUSINESS COMMUNITY

What Will It Take to Sustain Global Competitiveness?

I directed the development of the report *A Decade of Action* (BSCS 2007), which summarized recommendations from 20 contemporary reports published by a variety of business and industry groups, government agencies, and professional organizations. BSCS convened an expert panel and reviewed the reports for recommendations to science, technology, engineering, and mathematics (STEM) education in general, and specifically for K–12 science and technology education. The panel directed its attention to STEM education because the potential of these disciplines to contribute positively to education reform had not been fully recognized. Yet, the content and abilities of high-quality STEM education have clear and compelling connections to the goal of developing a 21st-century workforce and sustaining our global competitiveness.

Here is the general recommendation: To sustain the position of the United States as a global competitor, our nation needs a vision, a first tactical response, and a long-term strategic plan that outlines a decade of actions for reforming STEM education. Although the need to change seems evident, the changes specifically implied for K–12 STEM education must be clarified and addressed. The ability to address these changes presents one of the challenges for state, district, and school leaders.

How Can STEM Education Help the United States Rise Above the Gathering Storm?

In 2007, the National Academies published a report that immediately gained the nation's attention. *Rising Above the Gathering Storm: Educating and Employing America for a Brighter Economic Future* (NRC 2007a) brought together a distinguished committee that made a clear and compelling argument for changes in K–12 science and mathematics education so the United States could remain prosperous in the 21st century.

The chapter on K–12 science and mathematics education focused on *teachers* and the *students* they teach. The recommendations included the following:

- Annually recruit 10,000 science and mathematics teachers by awarding them four-year scholarships.
- Strengthen the skills of 250,000 teachers through summer institutes, master's programs, and Advanced Placement (AP) and International Baccalaureate (IB) training programs.
- Provide K–12 curriculum materials modeled on world-class standards.
- Enlarge the pipeline of students who are prepared to enter college and graduate with a degree in science, engineering, or mathematics.

In addition, the committee recommended two other strategies:

- Provide intensive learning experiences through statewide specialty high schools.
- Use inquiry-based learning to stimulate student interest and achievement in science, technology, engineering, and mathematics.

The primary disciplines emphasized for K–12 education were science and mathematics, and the emphasis was on those students destined for careers in science, engineering, and mathematics, as these disciplines were perceived as fundamental for technological innovation and economic productivity.

Are Scientists and Engineers in the Business Community Aware of STEM Education?

In 2010, the Entertainment and Media Communications Institute (E&MCI) reported a survey that examined the understanding and perception of the acronym *STEM*. The survey consisted of 5,011 participants from multiple organizations, most of which were STEM-based, such as aerospace and engineering societies. Results indicated that 86% of respondents were not familiar with the acronym STEM (E&MCI 2010). Because the sample consisted of individuals working in STEM-related fields, the results may be a concern for those entrusted with STEM education. From a branding perspective, this is not good, as the acronym likely does not convey a meaning to those beyond the policy makers and educators who are already involved with STEM education.

So one theme emerges again: For those interested in promoting STEM education at local, state, or national levels, it will be important to clarify and explain what STEM education means and why it is important. Historically, educators have not been good at the clarification and dissemination of reform initiatives. Contemporary STEM reform presents an opportunity to enhance the public's understanding of STEM education.

FEDERAL AND STATE GOVERNMENT PERSPECTIVES

What Will It Take for K–12 STEM Education to Prepare and Inspire Students?

In 2010, the President's Council of Advisors on Science and Technology (PCAST) presented President Obama with a report titled *Prepare and Inspire: K–12 Science, Technology, Engineering, and Math (STEM) Education for America's Future*. The thrust of the report centered on preparing all students to use STEM disciplines in their personal and working lives and inspiring them to pursue STEM careers.

The PCAST recommendations included the following:

- Prepare 100,000 STEM teachers over the next decade.
- Recognize excellence in STEM teaching by initiating a STEM Master Teacher Corps.
- Create an Advanced Research Projects Agency-Education (ARPA-Ed) that would harness the potential of technology.
- Increase the number of STEM-focused schools.
- Institute after-school programs that would provide students with connections across STEM disciplines.

What Would It Take for Students to Engage and Excel in Undergraduate Science, Technology, Engineering, and Mathematics Education?

In February 2012, PCAST released the report *Engage to Excel: Producing One Million Additional College Graduates With Degrees in Science, Technology, Engineering, and Mathematics*. Based on the projected need for STEM professionals, the report recommends strategies for improving STEM student recruitment and retention for the first two years of postsecondary education. Three imperatives establish a foundation for the report:

- Improve the first two years of STEM education in college.
- Provide all students with the tools to excel.
- Diversify pathways to STEM degrees.

The title *Engage to Excel* deserves a brief discussion. At a March 2012 meeting, I had a discussion with S. James Gates, Jr., a PCAST member and cochair of the report. Dr. Gates explained that the title applies to students, faculty, and leaders beyond colleges and universities. So, for example, students must be engaged to excel in STEM fields. Faculty members will excel if they engage in teaching methods based on research about why students excel and persist in STEM during the early years of college. Finally, success in achieving this goal depends on engagement by leaders at all levels, from those in colleges and universities to the president of the United States.

The report presents the following recommendations:

- Catalyze widespread adoption of empirically validated teaching practices.
- Advocate and provide support for replacing standard laboratory courses with discovery-based research courses.
- Launch a national experiment in postsecondary mathematics education to address the math preparation gap.
- Encourage partnerships among stakeholders to diversify pathways to STEM careers.
- Create a Presidential Council on STEM education with leadership from the academic and business communities to provide strategic leadership for transformative and sustainable change in STEM undergraduate education.

The theme and recommendations in this report hold some promise of improving the often-criticized college teaching. The changes seem reasonable and are based on research. The recommendations apply to K–12 STEM teachers as they would benefit from better models of teaching, discovery-based courses, sound mathematics, partnerships, and support from leaders.

What Would Be Addressed in a STEM Education Agenda?

The National Governors Association (NGA) published an update on state actions that address an education agenda for STEM (NGA 2011). The NGA has two goals: Increase the proficiency of all students in STEM, and increase the number of students who pursue advanced studies and careers. The stated reasons for the governors' goals are understandable and straightforward: STEM occupations are among the highest-paying, fastest-growing, and most essential jobs for economic growth and innovation.

The report lists the usual litany of reasons that U.S. education is in need of reform. Reasons include a lack of rigorous standards and assessments, poorly qualified teachers, lack of students prepared for postsecondary STEM study, a failure of schools to interest and motivate students, and a failure of postsecondary institutions to meet job demands in STEM fields.

So what is the STEM education agenda proposed by the governors? The list is fundamental and not surprising. States have taken these actions in light of the challenges:

- Adopt rigorous math and science standards and improved assessments.
- Recruit and retain more qualified classroom teachers and provide more rigorous preparation for STEM students.
- Incorporate informal learning opportunities to expand math and science beyond school programs.

- Enhance the quality and supply of STEM teachers.
- Establish goals of postsecondary institutions to meet job demands in STEM fields. (NGA 2011)

Although direct, the recommendations present clear policies for those working at the state level. The implications for the Common Core State Standards for Mathematics and English Language Arts and Literacy and the Next Generation Science Standards also seem understandable and acceptable.

THE EDUCATION COMMUNITY

Are Educators and Executives Aligned on the Creative Readiness of the U.S. Workforce?

In 2008, the Conference Board released *Ready to Innovate* (Lichtenberg, Woock, and Wright 2008), a report based on a survey of 155 U.S. business executives and 89 school superintendents. The point of the survey was to determine the skills and abilities that cultivate creativity—the abilities needed to compete in a business world of continual innovation, new technologies, and rapidly changing demands. Almost all of superintendents (99%) and employers (97%) agreed that creativity was of increasing importance in the workplace.

The survey asked respondents to identify skills that best demonstrate creativity. Employers indicated problem identification and superintendents indicated problem solving. Not surprisingly, degrees in the arts were rated the best educational indicators of creativity. The hard sciences and mathematics were rated the lowest indicators, with degrees in engineering and computer science in the mid-range of educators' evaluations.

Ready to Innovate (Lichtenberg, Woock, and Wright 2008) indicated that educators and executives were more aligned than not on the need for and attributes of creativity. Some of the top-ranked creative skills include the ability to take risks, problem identification and articulation, tolerance of ambiguity, and integration of knowledge across different disciplines. The general theme of innovation and this listing of abilities has implications for STEM education, especially consideration of school curricula and instruction.

Could STEM Education Provide Pathways to Prosperity?

Pathways to Prosperity, a report from the Harvard Graduate School of Education, was released in early 2011. The report builds a case from a more demanding labor market to the need for broader and deeper skills and insights from a global perspective on education reform. *Pathways to Prosperity* places considerable emphasis on the need to close the continually widening gap between demands of a 21st-century labor market and the interests and aspirations of 21st-century youth, especially minorities.

Several of the proposals in this report rest on the case that students cannot see connections between school programs and opportunities in the labor market. While avoiding explicit tracking, the report recommends developing connections between learning and work beginning in high school. Insights for these recommendations come from vocational education programs in northern and central Europe and especially from *Learning for Jobs* and *Jobs for Youth*, two reports from the Organisation for Economic Cooperation and Development (OECD 2009a; 2009b).

Work-based learning and career and technical education (CTE) programs are the pathways to prosperity that schools, especially high schools, should implement. Such programs would help adolescents and their families identify the patterns of course-taking and other experiences that would best position them for future careers.

There are direct implications for STEM, such as the engineering program Project Lead the Way and technology education programs, and indirect implications for science and mathematics education programs.

What Are Teachers' and Administrators' Perceptions of STEM Education?

The STEM education and leadership program at Illinois State University conducted a survey of 200 teachers and administrators (Brown, Brown, Reardon, and Merrill 2011). The survey was conducted to answer two questions: (1) Do administrators and STEM teachers have a basic understanding of STEM education? (2) What do administrators and STEM teachers believe about STEM education?

With regard to the first question, the authors concluded that STEM education is not well understood. Less than half of administrators understood STEM education—even though they had teachers in their building participating in a STEM-focused graduate program. Even teachers in STEM disciplines indicated varied levels of understanding of STEM education. In answering the second question, the team concluded that there is not a clear vision of STEM education even among those who support and teach STEM (Brown, Brown, Reardon, and Merrill 2011).

Although limited in scope, the implications of this research amplify the continuing need to clarify the form and function of STEM in education contexts and how STEM may be implemented in states, schools, and classrooms. The latter need is one purpose of this book.

Is STEM Education Slow Off the Mark?

Yes, according to a 2011 report from the Center for American Progress. The report is titled *Slow Off the Mark: Elementary School Teachers and the Crisis in Science, Technology, Engineering, and Math Education* (CAP 2011). The report makes a case for STEM education and the fact that elementary teachers are not prepared in STEM disciplines, especially science and mathematics. The background and rationale for the recommendations rest on the need to improve prospects for the future of U.S. global competitiveness.

The report makes five specific recommendations:

- Increase the selectivity of programs that prepare teachers for elementary grades.
- Implement teacher compensation policies, including performance-based pay, that make elementary teaching a more attractive career for college graduates and career-changers with strong STEM backgrounds.
- Include more mathematics and science content and pedagogy in schools of education.
- Require candidates to pass mathematics and science subsections of licensure exams.
- Explore innovative staffing models that extend the reach of elementary-level

teachers with an affinity for mathematics and science and demonstrated effectiveness in teaching them.

Can More Time Strengthen STEM Education?

The 2011 report from the National Center on Time & Learning (NCTL), *Strengthening Science Education: The Power of More Time to Deepen Inquiry and Engagement*, suggests the likely answer is yes. The report presents a positive answer for science education, and I think it is reasonable to extend that answer to STEM education, whether it is approached as separate or integrated disciplines.

For many, the call for more time is often a first recommendation, an "easy call" for efforts to improve student outcomes. This report goes beyond the easy call. NCTL reviewed results from five public elementary schools that lengthened the school day and instituted a goal of improving science instruction.

The rationale for increasing time on science instruction was poor achievement on the National Assessment of Educational Progress (NAEP), Trends in International Mathematics and Science Study (TIMSS), and Program for International Student Assessment (PISA), combined with the need for more college graduates in STEM disciplines and a greater representation of women and people of color in STEM jobs. The decline in science proficiency threatens the nation's economic competitiveness and potential to solve pressing problems in domains such as energy, health, and the environment.

The NCTL report presents data supporting the observation that time for science instruction in elementary schools has declined since the No Child Left Behind legislation. The report appeals to contemporary reports such as *Taking Science to School* (NRC 2007b) and the need to increase student engagement and competence in science. Achieving these goals will require more instructional time to teach and learn science and more time for professional development to build teachers' knowledge and skills.

The schools profiled in this report are a mix of urban and rural. All five schools have majority high-poverty student populations, and several had significant groups of students whose first language is not English. A very important note is that students in four of the five schools demonstrated gains in science proficiency on science assessments.

The results of this study clearly support the implication that more time in the school day—and likely in the school year—will strengthen students' competencies in STEM disciplines. It is equally clear that more time to do the same thing is not the conclusion of the report. Along with more time, the schools

- incorporated more hands-on activities and encouraged more scientific discourse;
- implemented specific strategies to counter deficiencies in reading levels, contexts, and vocabulary;
- embellished core content with connections to careers; and
- enhanced school programs with experiences in informal settings.

In addition, leaders in the schools made sure that teachers' capacities were strengthened through professional development that

- focused on improving content knowledge and pedagogical skills,
- used assessment data to improve instruction, and
- ensured the core curriculum was aligned with schools and classrooms and mapped to district and state standards and assessments. (NCTL 2011)

I found the report in general, and the case studies in particular, very exciting. They presented extensive proof that an initiative such as more time can make a difference and that reform suggested by STEM can result in higher levels of achievement by diverse populations of students. The observation that more time meant changes in curriculum, instruction, and assessments, and that these changes were supported by professional development, provided insights that need attention from those addressing the challenges and opportunities of STEM education.

What About STEM Learning After School?

Informal and after-school experiences are often overlooked as the education community considers how to improve students' learning, attitudes, and career choices, but these experiences should not be overlooked.

In 2011, the Afterschool Alliance published the report *STEM Learning in Afterschool: An Analysis of Impact and Outcomes.* Leading with a justification based on racial and ethnic equality and the need to increase the representation of women and minorities in STEM fields, the report argues that after-school programs, including before-school and summer programs, are well placed to help close the opportunity gap faced by many underserved and underrepresented groups.

The group reviewed evaluations of after-school programs and reported STEM-specific benefits in these broad categories:

- improved attitudes toward STEM fields and careers,
- increased STEM knowledge and skills, and
- higher likelihood of graduation and pursuit of STEM careers (Afterschool Alliance 2011).

The report includes brief summaries of numerous programs across the country and provides supporting data for the benefits of after-school programs.

Are There Examples of Successful K–12 STEM Education?

The answer is yes. In 2011, the NRC published *Successful K–12 STEM Education,* a report that identified effective STEM schools and programs and clarifying criteria that could be addressed with available data. The goal of this NRC report is to provide information that leaders at national, state, and school levels can use to make strategic decisions about improving STEM education (NRC 2011; see aso *Monitoring Progress Toward Successful K–12 STEM Education : A Nation Advancing* [BOSE 2013]).

The report focused its analysis on the science and mathematics components of STEM. Furthermore, the primary emphasis was on successful STEM schools. The criteria for identifying successful STEM schools included student outcomes, specifications for STEM focus, and school-level practices and instruction. The report included brief case studies and examples of STEM schools and programs.

This NRC report found that effective STEM instruction engages students' interests and experiences, identifies and builds on their knowledge, uses STEM practices, and provides experiences that sustain their interest (NRC 2011; BOSE 2013). The report also helpfully identified key elements that provided the foundation for effective STEM instruction. Those elements included

- a coherent set of standards and curriculum,
- teachers with high capacity to teach this discipline,
- a supportive system of assessment and accountability,
- adequate instructional time, and
- equal access to high-quality STEM learning opportunities. (NRC 2011)

The report concludes with recommendations for schools, districts, states, and national policy makers with intentions to support effective K–12 STEM education. Those recommendations are largely related to the aforementioned elements supporting effective instruction.

Are There Insights From a 2011 National Survey on STEM Education?

In 2011, Interactive Educational Systems Design, Inc. (IESD), conducted an online survey of K–12 STEM leaders in districts and schools. The response rate included 515 total respondents, with more than 400 responding to most survey questions. Despite the relatively low response rate, I found the findings insightful and informative for those leading STEM initiatives.

Findings from this survey included the following:

- Just more than 62% (62.1%) of respondents reported use of one or more programs that integrate core concepts of STEM.
- A majority of respondents reported offering career and technical education programs (66.7%), introduction to technology courses (63.6%), and computer science and programming courses (61.1%).
- A majority indicated that their districts or schools currently offered or were likely to offer robotics (65.6%), engineering fundamentals (57.6%), and energy and the environment courses (57.4%) in the next one to three years.
- About half of the respondents reported that their districts or schools either currently offered or were very likely to offer middle school STEM courses (52.9%) and elementary-level STEM courses (46.2%) in the next one to three years. (IESD 2011)

The IESD survey also identified challenges facing STEM education. The insights here are informative but not surprising. The three most significant challenges are

- insufficient funding specifically designated for STEM (74.0%),
- low number of qualified STEM teachers (55.9%), and
- insufficient professional development for STEM teachers (54.6%). (IESD 2011)

Yes, these are insights from this survey. Those engaged in STEM education should be encouraged by the findings. Furthermore, those concerned with specific types of courses, challenges, role of technologies such as e-books, and projections for professional development should find the detailed results informative.

THE PARENTS' AND PUBLIC'S PERSPECTIVE

Relative to STEM Education, Are Parents and the Public Beginning to See the Light?

In 2010, Public Agenda completed a survey of more than 1,400 individuals, including 646 parents of students in grades K–12. The survey report is called *Are We Beginning to See the Light?* The survey results indicated broad support from parents and the general public for K–12 national standards; more than half of parents (52%) say the math and science education their child currently receives in school is "fine as it is" (Public Agenda 2010).

Survey results also indicate that the general public favors a national curriculum as one way to improve STEM education: Eight in ten Americans say establishing a national curriculum in math would improve STEM education, with more than half (53%) saying it would improve it a lot. Additionally, 78% indicate the same about national curriculum in science, with 48% saying it would improve STEM education a lot. (Note the lack of response about technology and engineering curriculum.)

Many parents surveyed said they also would like to see their local schools spend more money on up-to-date and well-equipped science labs (70%), more equipment for hands-on learning (69%), and more equipment to help students learn computer and technology skills (68%). The majority of parents with children in grades 6–12 say they want to see more emphasis in their child's school on STEM topics such as computer programming (65%), basic engineering principles (52%), and statistics and probability (49%).

While only 30% of Americans see a demand for science- and math-focused jobs in the current economy, 84% agree that there will be a lot more jobs in the future that require math and science skills. Also, nine out of ten Americans say studying advanced math and science is useful even for students who do not pursue a STEM career. Additionally, 88% of the public agrees that students with advanced math and science skills will have an advantage when it comes to college opportunities.

In reviewing the survey's items, it is clear that the economy and jobs were linked to schools and STEM, especially science and math.

How Can STEM Education Inspire the Next Generations of Doctors, Scientists, Software Developers, and Engineers?

Microsoft Corporation commissioned a national survey that included parents of K–12 students. Harris Interactive conducted the survey, titled *STEM Perceptions: Student and Parent Study* (Harris 2011). The survey reflected the PCAST report, in that it was designed to gain insights about how to better prepare and inspire students to pursue postsecondary education in STEM subjects.

There were three important insights from the parents:

1. A majority of parents of K–12 students (93%) believe that STEM education *should* be a priority in the U.S. However, only about half (49%) agree that STEM education actually *is* a priority for this country.

2. Parents who report that STEM should be a priority present as justification the need to ensure the United States remains competitive in the global marketplace (53%) and to produce the next generation of innovators (51%).

3. Although half of parents (50%) would like to see their children pursue STEM careers, only a small percentage (24%) are very willing to spend extra money helping their children with math and science. (Harris Interactive 2011)

This survey did not define STEM, and thus it is likely that many respondents had varied and probably mostly science-centric views of what STEM education is.

CONCLUSION

Clearly, the questions varied. Beginning with Secretary Duncan's rationale, the implied question for the business community was, "What do we need for a knowledge economy?" Variations on answers to this question included sustaining global competitiveness, maintaining the workforce, brightening our economic future, and securing America's future in general. The theme of jobs and the economy across the reports was not surprising, and *Rising Above the Gathering Storm* (NRC 2007a) signaled the worst economic times since the Great Depression.

Scientists, engineers, and school administrators are not clear about STEM education. Even some administrators with STEM programs in their schools are not clear about the meaning of the acronym. Amid the ambiguity, if not confusion, relative to STEM education are recommendations for more schools, teachers, curricula, and professional developments for STEM.

There is a need to examine the different perspectives on STEM education. That said, I do not think there is one defining meaning for the acronym. Several meanings already exist. Perhaps the most reasonable approach is to clarify the options for those educators who are initiating a new STEM program or improving an existing one.

I will conclude with one important observation: The majority of reports addressed science and mathematics and gave little or no recognition to technology and engineering.

DISCUSSION QUESTIONS

1. If STEM education is the answer, how would you formulate the question?

2. How would you explain the use of STEM by so many diverse groups?

3. What role might the many reports have on programs for STEM education?

4. In general, the reports made recommendations for science and mathematics. Would technology and engineering have been appropriate to include? If so, how and why?

CHAPTER 6

If STEM Is an Opportunity, What Is the Federal Government's Role?

I n December 2009, I participated in a planning meeting of the President's Council of Advisors on Science and Technology (PCAST). The purpose of the meeting was to formulate an agenda for a PCAST report concerning the federal investment in science, technology, engineering, and mathematics (STEM) education. That report was published as *Prepare and Inspire: K–12 Science, Technology, Engineering and Math (STEM) Education for America's Future* (PCAST 2010). The report is summarized in Chapter 5 (p. 43). Although prior work had focused on the federal role, preparation for the December 2009 meeting directed my interest to STEM education as a theme, especially for national policy makers.

This chapter first describes a 2010 mandate for federal agencies to prepare a five-year strategic plan for STEM education. I then present my priorities for such a plan. These recommendations are followed by a general discussion of the federal role in improving STEM education.

A STRATEGIC PLAN FOR FEDERAL INVESTMENT IN STEM EDUCATION

This discussion centers on a mandate from Congress to the Office of Science and Technology Policy (OSTP). Here is the mandate:

> The National Science and Technology Council's Committee on STEM
> Education (a list of agencies on the committee is included below) within the
> Office of Science and Technology Policy (OSTP) is required by the America
> COMPETES Reauthorization Act of 2010 to develop a five-year federal science,
> technology, engineering, and mathematics (STEM) education strategic plan by
> early 2012. The plan will guide all federal investment in formal (preK through
> graduate school) and informal (beyond the school walls) STEM education.
> (OSTP 2011)

The National Science and Technology Council (NSTC) is an internal government group consisting of various departments and agencies. PCAST consists of members outside the government. Both NSTC and PCAST advise OSTP. The agencies on the STEM education committee are listed in Figure 6.1 (p. 54).

Figure 6.1: Federal Agencies on the STEM Education Committee

Office of Science and Technology Policy (OSTP) (co-chair)

National Institute of Standards and Technology (NIST) (co-chair)

National Science Foundation (NSF) (co-chair)

Department of Agriculture

Department of Commerce

Department of Defense

Department of Education

Department of Energy

Department of Health and Human Services

Department of Interior

Department of Transportation

Environmental Protection Agency

National Aeronautics and Space Administration (NASA)

An Inventory of STEM Initiatives

The strategic plan includes a survey and inventory of the investments that federal agencies have made in STEM education. Specifically, OSTP created an interagency committee that cataloged all federal investments in STEM education and analyzed the amount of duplication, overlap, and fragmentation in agency programs. The inventory was completed late in 2011 and released in early 2012 in *Description of 5-Year Federal STEM Education Strategies Plan: Report to Congress* (OSTP 2011). This inventory was very detailed and thorough in organizing agencies' activities, programs, and investments. One finding was, in my view, particularly important. This finding did not discuss whether investments were too large or too small or whether there was too much overlap and redundancy. Rather, the primary issue was how to strategically focus federal dollars so that we would have a significant impact in areas of national priority (OSTP 2011). Here is a summary of specific results from the inventory:

- Federal agencies are making 252 distinct investments in STEM education.
- The total budgetary investment is $3.4 billion.
- Of the $3.4 billion spent on STEM education, $967 million (28%) is targeted to specific workforce needs of science mission agencies.
- There is spending of $2.5 billion (72%) on broader STEM education. Expenditures

of the National Science Foundation (NSF) and Department of Education ($1.2 billion and $1 billion, respectively) dominate the support of broader STEM education.

- There are $1.1 billion in investments directed toward groups that are underrepresented in STEM.
- An investment of $312 million (spread across 24 investments) has a primary goal of improving teacher effectiveness, mostly through teacher professional development. (OSTP 2011)

Although these investments seem like substantial amounts of money, an overall perspective may help. The federal investment in STEM education (i.e., $3.4 billion) is less than 1% of the $1.1 trillion spent on education annually in the United States.

I return to the primary issue of strategically focusing federal funds so they will have the maximum impact on national priorities. There is remarkable potential if the Federal agencies are able to develop coherent, coordinated, and focused initiatives with high value for short- and long-term returns (i.e., five years and decades) and center on national priorities (i.e., STEM literacy for citizens, workforce skills and abilities, and STEM careers).

Finally, and very important in this era of constrained budgets, the current expenditures of $3.4 billion per year could be redirected and coordinated by addressing strategic priorities for the improvement of STEM education. Do I think this would be easy? No. But it may be possible, and that is my reason for addressing this national challenge for STEM education. Although it is possible, I must admit the probability of this happening is very small.

A Long-Range Strategic Plan

To be truthful, I am most interested in the long-range strategic plan. The difference between the survey and plan is a distinction between the immediate and concrete results of the inventory and the potential to improve STEM education.

Understandably, the strategic plan should include the aims and goals that the plan is designed to achieve. An essential part of this aspect of the survey must be a clarification of what STEM education means for this strategic plan. A place to begin might be the purpose of STEM literacy presented in the introduction. Second, the plan should describe criteria for the design of STEM programs—that is, what states, schools, and teachers will need. What research should be used as the basis for STEM programs? Third, the plan requires the inclusion of evaluation research to complement the development and implementation of the various STEM programs. Fourth, the strategic plan must include a short list of priorities—for example, between three and five initiatives that federal government agencies could reasonably pursue. The potential for these initiatives to make a difference relative to the stated goals should be extremely high. Finally, the plan should delineate the who, what, when, and where of getting the plan from initial efforts to final implementation.

This list is not necessarily profound or insightful. Rather, it is fundamental, practical, and (I hope) reasonable. What follows is a discussion of the orientation and justification for the priorities. I then outline and provide a follow-up discussion that includes further justification and some details of the recommendations.

I will begin with the three goals for the plan. The strategic plan must advance STEM education with the purpose of contributing to

- a STEM-literate society,
- a deep technical workforce for the 21st century, and
- an advanced research and development workforce.

Relative to K–12 education, these three goals should direct any strategic plan, whether at the national, state, or local levels. The first and second goals relate to all students as future citizens and members of the workforce. The third goal applies to those students who will continue their education by pursuing STEM-related careers.

Being Strategic in the Strategic Plan

To say the least, STEM education presents an array of definitions, perspectives, and orientations. Depending on the individuals, group, or agency, STEM education may refer to precollege or college levels, formal or informal contexts, traditional disciplines or integrated curriculum, public understanding or a pipeline agenda, or other diverse references. By definition, a strategic plan identifies priorities for those areas that are effective in achieving the stated goals—in this case, higher levels of STEM literacy, enhanced technical abilities, and a strengthened community of scientists, engineers, and mathematicians. Clearly, one approach will not provide an adequate plan. Any strategic plan for STEM education should address the multiple components of STEM education.

It may help to use an ecosystem metaphor. Recall that an ecosystem is a community of different species interacting with one another and the physical (i.e., abiotic, or nonliving) environment. An ecosystem may vary in size (e.g., a pond or a forest, depending on the unit of study). The parameters of an ecosystem can be defined by the study with specific boundaries, components, and resources. In reality, ecosystems are not distinct units. The application of the ecosystems metaphor to STEM education can be for states, school districts, or schools, for example. What are the living (e.g., teachers, students) and nonliving (e.g., instructional materials, hardware, software) features that are interrelated and interact? What are the areas or parameters of the interactions (e.g., national, state, school districts)? What are the material and information resources that flow into the system? What are the indicators of the system's health, vitality, and sustainability or decline?

In the complex ecology of STEM education, I suggest focusing resources on the instructional core of practice. I have discussed this idea in *The Teaching of Science: 21st-Century Perspectives* (Bybee 2010). The idea of an instructional core is adapted from the work of Richard Elmore (2009). The instructional core consists of the content and competencies that students are taught: Think of national and state standards and the teachers' knowledge and skills; think of teacher education and professional development and students' engagement and active learning; think of curriculum and instruction.

So, to be strategic, the plan should focus on means to engage students and enhance learning relative to the aforementioned goals, provide teachers with the knowledge and skills needed to enhance learning, and incorporate the content and competencies aligned with the goals of STEM education. My recommendations for a strategic plan follow from this discussion.

RECOMMENDATIONS FOR A FIVE-YEAR FEDERAL STEM EDUCATION STRATEGIC PLAN

Following are five initiatives that I recommend for a federal strategic plan. These priorities present broad perspectives that address the goal of improving U.S. STEM education in grades K–12. The initiatives are given with a succinct clarification. Rather than review the issues and needs, I describe some essential features of the priorities. Later sections elaborate details of the recommendations.

Priority 1: Develop a New Generation of Models and Tools for STEM Education.

Design specifications for these instructional materials include (1) using core concepts aligned with common core math standards, the Next Generation Science Standards, and standards for technology literacy; (2) providing a coherent framework for horizontal (i.e., grade levels) and vertical (i.e., K–12 programs) articulation; (3) incorporating contemporary research on how students learn; (4) aligning materials with key themes from international, national, and state standards and assessments; (5) emphasizing scientific practices, technological and engineering design, and mathematical practices as features of the programs; (6) using key personal and social contexts for the integration of STEM disciplines; and (7) facilitating development of 21st-century skills.

The models and tools for new instructional materials should include several programs for each grade-level set (e.g., elementary school), incorporate educational technologies (e.g., use of e-books, games, simulations), and address the needs for all students (e.g., college and career).

The NSF should lead this initiative, as it has more than 50 years of history in such efforts. With design specifications for the instructional materials in place, the work of federal agencies could focus on different topics, grade levels, and other areas. For the instructional units, Table 6.1 (p. 58) presents examples of federal agencies and possible themes for instructional units. Note the absence of the U.S. Department of Education in the table; this is due to a restriction on developing instructional materials and my recommendation that the U.S. Department of Education play a key role in the professional development of teachers based on these instructional materials.

The development and dissemination of the units could be modeled after the work of the National Institutes of Health (NIH), Office of Science Education. Under the leadership of Dr. Bruce Fuchs, the NIH Office of Science Education coordinated units on a variety of topics identified by the NIH institutes and developed by professional curriculum teams at the Biological Sciences Curriculum Study (BSCS) and the Education Development Center (EDC).

Priority 2: Support Professional Development of STEM Teachers.

A couple of specific actions are recommended to achieve this goal:

1. Establish summer institutes of two weeks' duration with follow-up of at least six days during the academic year to focus on building teachers' content and pedagogical knowledge and skills.

2. Develop online communities to support all participating teachers. These professional development programs should be concentrated and continuous; have an educational context; focus on content; and establish a learning community within the state, district, or school.

Table 6.1. Federal Agencies and Possible Themes for Model Instructional Materials

Department	Instructional unit theme
Department of Agriculture	21st-century green revolution
Department of Commerce	Green jobs and careers
Department of Defense	Technical systems
Department of Energy	Energy efficiency
Department of Health and Human Services	Health
Department of Interior	Resource use
Department of Transportation	Fuel-efficiency of cars
Environmental Protection Agency (EPA)	Environmental quality
National Aeronautics and Space Administration (NASA)	Research frontiers in space
National Oceanic and Atmosphere Administration (NOAA)	Climate change

To satisfy these criteria, the professional development programs should provide enough initial time to establish a clear foundation for teaching and learning. In addition to a concentration, the program should extend over the course of a year and include continuous work on improving curriculum, instruction, and classroom assessments. The educational context for the programs may include curriculum models—that is, content and pedagogy with direct and purposeful meaning for teachers. Core concepts and practices of science, technology, engineering, and mathematics must be the programs' focus. Finally, the programs require the establishment of professional learning communities with teams of teachers analyzing teaching, engaging in lesson study, reviewing content, and working on the implementation of instructional materials.

The Department of Education should lead this initiative, as it has a history of Mathematics and Science Partnerships (MSP) and it would not be a stretch to redirect those funds to STEM partnerships.

The initial work of the institutes and professional development should concentrate on the model instructional units, as these would be concrete examples of the innovations that form the basis of a STEM education reform. I am referring to innovations such as common standards for states; research on learning; emphasis on science, technology, engineering, and mathematics practices; and 21st-century workforce skills.

Priority 3: Align State Certification and Accreditation of STEM Teachers With Contemporary National Priorities.

This recommendation uses the critical leverage of teacher certification to facilitate reform of undergraduate teacher education programs. No discussion of improving STEM education escapes acknowledging the need to change teacher education. This includes changes in states' certification and national accreditation (e.g., Teacher Education Accreditation Council [TEAC]). In addition, federal support to colleges and universities that prepare significant numbers of future STEM teachers will be a major contribution to the reform. To this recommendation, I would add special support to colleges and universities with significant populations of Hispanic, African American, and Native American students so those institutions can recruit and prepare a more diverse group of STEM teachers.

With support from the federal government, this initiative should be coordinated with organizations such as the Council of Chief State School Officers (CCSSO), the Council for Accreditation of Educator Preparation (CAEP), and organizations that regularly convene state leaders, such as Achieve and Education Commission of the States (ECS).

Priority 4: Build District-Level Capacity for Continuous Improvement of STEM Education.

The specific actions necessary for this priority include

- developing teams of leaders who have the responsibility of curriculum reform;
- providing summer programs and technical assistance during the academic year;
- centering on critical leverage points, such as the selection of new instructional materials; and
- designing the programs so the district builds an infrastructure that is sustainable over time.

This priority connects to priorities 1, 2, and 3, with the goal of sustaining the initial results attained through curriculum reform, professional development, and alignment of policies. Although the federal costs may be high initially, by building district-level capacity, one could anticipate reduced support in the long term.

This initiative could be a part of the STEM partnership program described in Priority 2. The Department of Education might facilitate the program, but funding and coordination would occur at the state level.

Priority 5: Explain to the Public What STEM Education Is and Why It Will Benefit Their Children and the Nation.

One of the great insights from the Sputnik era was the fact that national leaders provided clear and compelling explanations of what the reform was and why it was important. Furthermore, there was continued support for science teachers and a national enthusiasm for reform. For example, proclamations such as "I am teaching science as inquiry" or "We are preparing science teachers for BSCS programs" echoed throughout the schools and colleges of this country.

The leadership for this part of the strategic plan should come from the White House and be delivered by the president and the President's Office of Science and Technology (OSTP) and leaders in federal agencies and associated STEM education committees and coalitions.

This is a low-cost, high-value initiative, one that has not been clear since the Sputnik era. The importance of a nonmilitary national mission and positive aspirations for the future could be invaluable to the American public. It also is the case that STEM education could make clear and direct connections to the public through topics such as health, environmental quality, resource use, and energy efficiency.

These recommendations have some important features. First, they center on critical leverage points in addressing immediate and long-term national problems. Second, the direct implications for the federal government involve financial support versus unfunded mandates; requests for cooperation; general recommendations to state and local governments; and appeals for support from business, industry, or private foundations. Third, priorities include multiple and coordinated efforts among, for example, the U.S. Department of Education, the National Science Foundation (NSF), the National Institutes of Health (NIH), and other government agencies. Fourth, where possible, the initiatives should build on current research, such as *How Students Learn: Science in the Classroom* (Donovan and Bransford 2005), *America's Lab Report,* (NRC 2006), and *Taking Science to School* (NRC 2007b). Finally, the responsibility for developing and implementing the federal strategy can support these priorities from a nonpartisan perspective. It is in the country's best interest to achieve higher levels of STEM literacy for all citizens, develop a technologically competent workforce, and recruit and prepare more scientists and engineers, especially from underrepresented groups.

Some Reflections on Improving STEM Education and the Federal Role

The federal government already spends $3.4 billion dollars each year on education initiatives, many of which are variations of those suggested in the five recommendations just presented.

The recommendations are informed by a rationale to keep funding for STEM priorities close to those areas that matter most when it comes to the significant indicator of success— student achievement. What matters most? Common standards, competent teachers, coherent curricula, and assessments aligned with standards and curricula.

Now, the development of common standards that include the STEM disciplines presents one of the great opportunities in American STEM education. This is especially true when one includes the development of assessments by large numbers of states. Capitalizing on this opportunity with the tools teachers need—exemplary models and tools for instructional materials and professional development focusing on content and pedagogy—seems obvious, at least to me.

The Next Generation Science Standards engage teachers' request for instructional materials to help them teach to the standards and some assurance that state standards and assessment are indeed aligned. Models of instructional materials designed to accommodate the common core math and Next Generation Science Standards do not exist, and only a select number of organizations have the capacity to create exemplary models and tools. The federal government could coordinate efforts among agencies to initiate development of a series of units that respond to STEM teachers' requests for materials to help them do their jobs. Such an effort would bring greater coherence to STEM programs and represent the priorities of different federal agencies. They would not present a national curriculum. The considerable expenditure that federal agencies currently direct toward instructional materials could be redirected to the design, development, and implementation of a variety of models that exemplify a new generation for STEM education.

The second recommendation extends from the first: Use the exemplary instructional units as the basis for the professional development of those STEM teachers already in classrooms as well as those in teacher education programs. Again, the federal agencies support various workshops, partnerships, and institutes that could be coordinated in support of STEM education, and the aforementioned instructional units could be used as the basis for updating STEM content and effective pedagogy, enhancing their understanding of learning, and aligning curriculum and instruction with assessment.

If STEM reform is to be successful, it must extend beyond new standards, teachers, and updated materials. Building the capacity for sustainable reform requires the involvement of school, district, and state administrations and the alignment of teacher certifications, graduation requirements, and state assessments. The federal government can facilitate work at these levels and help build capacity in the larger infrastructure of the education system.

Finally, the general public does not understand the STEM disciplines; their practices; or their relationship to innovation, economic development, and national progress. Unfortunately, this lack of understanding includes many within the education system. The reasons for advancing STEM education are clear and compelling to those interested in advancing STEM education; now it is time to make the reasons clear to policy makers, school personnel, and STEM teachers. There is an equally clear and compelling need to explain to the public why advancing STEM education will help establish new national aspirations and educate a new generation of STEM-literate citizens, prepare a 21st-century workforce, and maintain U.S. research and development capacity with diverse and competent scientists, technologists, engineers, and mathematicians.

CONCLUSION

This chapter addresses the federal role in STEM education and the improvement of STEM education. Specifically, the chapter outlines five priorities that could be considered as a response to a mandated five-year strategic plan for STEM education. The priorities I recommended are as follows:

1. Develop a new generation of models and tools for STEM education.
2. Support professional development for STEM teachers.
3. Align state certification and accreditation of STEM teachers.
4. Build district-level capacity for continuous improvement of STEM education.
5. Explain to the public what STEM education is and why it will benefit children and the nation.

DISCUSSION QUESTIONS

1. What would you consider an appropriate (or inappropriate) role of the federal government for improving STEM education?
2. What would you propose as priorities for a five-year strategic plan to improve STEM education in your state, district, or school?
3. How would you evaluate the success of the five-year strategic plan at the federal level? State level? District level? School level?

How Can a State, District, or School Develop a Coherent Strategy for STEM Education?

Chapter 5 presented the issue—STEM education seems to be the answer. What was the question? A review of education references and contemporary reports revealed themes such as global problems, economic progress, and advanced scientific and technological innovations as the reasons for proposing STEM education as a national priority.

This chapter identifies a general question about the purposes of STEM education. Proposing answers to the question sets the stage for leaders to develop a strategy for advancing STEM education. Let's begin with a question. How can education help develop

- a STEM-literate society,
- a deep technical workforce for the 21st-century's knowledge economics, and
- an advanced research and development workforce focused on innovation?

This question tops the nation's STEM agenda. Of course, the general question must be translated to states, school districts, schools, and ultimately classrooms and teachers. The next sections are a first brief look at the three aspects of the question—STEM literacy for all citizens, a 21st-century workforce, and individuals pursuing advanced research and development careers.

A STEM-LITERATE SOCIETY

How can educators contribute to STEM literacy? The first thing to understand in answering this question is that it likely requires a change in perceptions about STEM literacy. The answer might begin with separate STEM courses. This would be the traditional view. Or the answer might progress to integrated courses. Regardless, the 21st-century STEM view requires students as future citizens to apply knowledge from the STEM disciplines to life situations. Table 7.1 (p. 64) summarizes examples of contexts for personal and social perspectives for STEM education.

This discussion elaborates on the earlier aim for STEM education and answers a second question: How is STEM literacy different from scientific, technological, engineering, or mathematical literacy?

Table 7.1. Contexts for STEM Education

Global, national, and local issues	Health maintenance and disease prevention Energy efficiency Environmental quality Natural hazards Natural resource use Understanding of STEM disciplines
Educational theme	A STEM-literate society
Advancing the goals of STEM education	Address 21st-century grand challenges in appropriate programs, courses, and classes Provide opportunities for the applications of knowledge and skills to STEM-related issues Include scientific, engineering, design, and mathematical Practices

A Definition of STEM Literacy

We can begin the discussion with a definition. My work on the Program for International Student Assessment (PISA) has influenced this formulation of STEM literacy (see OECD 2006; OECD 2009; Bybee and McCrae 2009). Figure 7.1 presents a proposed definition of STEM literacy.

This discussion of STEM literacy begins with the assertion that the primary purpose of STEM education is not solely and exclusively mastery of subject matter in respective STEM disciplines. Of course, STEM literacy includes the basic science, technology, engineering, and mathematics concepts and processes, but it must go beyond this traditional discipline-bound view. Rather, it should center on education that consists of the general learning of all citizens. In general, this is the Greek idea of *paideia*. Although understanding foundational subject matter in the sciences, technology, engineering, and mathematics is essential, one must consider the use and application of that knowledge, not just the acquisition of knowledge as a primary purpose of STEM education.

Future Scientists, Technologists, Engineers, and Mathematicians

There should be a clear distinction between an education in science that prepares for future study of science, for example, and an education that contributes to students' growth into literate adults. As literate adults, individuals should be competent to understand STEM-related global issues; recognize scientific from other nonscientific explanations; make reasonable arguments based on evidence; and, very important, fulfill their civic duties at the local, national, and global levels.

The idea that the purpose of education should center on full development of students as future citizens is quite old. In contemporary discussions of *Global Crises, Global Solutions* (Lomborg 2004), one can identify the purpose of STEM education with the following quote:

> Defining scope of the problem of "lack of education" must begin with the
> *objectives* of education—which is to equip people with a range of competencies

> **Figure 7.1. A Definition of STEM Literacy**
>
> STEM literacy refers to an individual's
>
> - knowledge, attitudes, and skills to identify questions and problems in life situations, to explain the natural and designed world, and to draw evidence-based conclusions about STEM related-issues;
> - understanding of the characteristic features of STEM disciplines as forms of human knowledge, inquiry, and design;
> - awareness of how STEM disciplines shape our material, intellectual, and cultural environments; and
> - willingness to engage in STEM-related issues and with the ideas of science, technology, engineering, and mathematics as a constructive, concerned, and reflective citizen.

(which include both cognitive and non-cognitive skills, knowledge and attitudes) necessary to lead productive, fulfilling lives fully integrated into their societies and communities. (Pritchett in Lomborg 2004, p. 175)

This quote introduces competencies to describe a range of knowledge, attitudes, and skills that individuals should develop. It does not, however, elaborate on specific knowledge, attitudes, or skills; the latter is one challenge of STEM education.

A STEM Perspective for Public Education

In *Public Education* (1976), historian Lawrence Cremin proposed an ecological perspective that "views educational institutions and configurations in the relation to one another and to the larger society that sustains them and is in turn affected by them" (Cremin 1976, p. 36) as a useful perspective for describing education issues and a theme such as STEM education. Cremin includes both formal education (i.e., schooling) and informal education (i.e., media, museums, churches, and synagogues). Also, note that Cremin underscores the connection between education institutions and larger society, a prominent theme of this discussion of STEM education.

One aspect of STEM literacy is to help individuals develop a sense of social, political, and ethical aspirations. Cremin provides a key point for the theme of STEM education:

> How, then do we achieve an appropriate balance between the demands of individuality and the demands of community? I have a very simple starting point to which I think there is no alternative. We converse—informally in small groups and more formally through organizations via systematic political processes. The proper education of the public and indeed the proper creation of "publics" will

not go forward in our society until we undertake anew a great public dialogue about education are among the most important questions that can be raised in our society, particularly at this juncture in its history. (Cremin 1976, p. 74)

Although written almost four decades ago, Cremin's theme of balancing the demands of both individuals and communities applies to this consideration of STEM literacy. His advice to begin a great public dialogue is just one more reason I had for writing this book. At the least, the book should facilitate discourse about STEM within the education community.

A DEEP TECHNICAL WORKFORCE

This aim includes all students, not just those destined to careers in science, technology, engineering, and mathematics. The skills described here apply to all 21st-century careers. Activities in science, technology, engineering, and mathematics lessons and courses provide many opportunities to develop the skills needed for a deep technical workforce. Table 7.2 summarizes this aim for STEM education.

Table 7.2. STEM Education and 21st-Century Skills

National issue	Knowledge economy
Education theme	A deep technical workforce
Advancing the goals of STEM education	Develop students 21st-century skills and abilities: • Adaptability • Complex communication • Nonroutine problem solving • Self-management/self-development • Systems thinking

As we observed in Chapter 5 in the review of contemporary reports, there is continued reference to developing capacities such as intellectual skills, cognitive abilities, scientific reasoning, and problem solving—in short, a deep technical workforce. Such abilities should be fundamental as we consider STEM programs, teacher education, and professional development. Unfortunately, the development of cognitive abilities is often assumed to be either a frivolous embellishment or a collateral outcome that occurs concomitantly with an education filled with the memorization of meaningless information. Developing the mental processes of scientific inquiry and engineering design, for example, is the direct outcome of engaging students in appropriate experiences that require the practice and application of such cognitive abilities. STEM educators know how to design programs that provide students opportunities to achieve these aims while developing a deep and rich understanding of basic scientific, technological, engineering, and mathematical ideas.

21st-Century Skills

What skills and abilities should be included in STEM programs? Figure 7.2 describes recommendations for 21st-century skills. These skills are adapted from *Exploring the Intersection of Science Education and 21st-Century Skills* (NRC 2010).

Figure 7.2. Skills for a Deep Technical Workforce

1. **Adaptability**: The ability and willingness to cope with uncertain, new, and rapidly changing conditions on the job, including responding effectively to emergencies or crisis situations and learning new tasks, technologies, and procedures.

   Adaptability also includes handling work stress; adapting to different personalities, communication styles, and cultures; and physical adaptability to various indoor or outdoor work environments (Houston 2007; Pulakos, Arad, Donnovan, and Plamondon 2000).

2. **Complex communications and social skills**: Skills in processing and interpreting both verbal and nonverbal information from others to respond appropriately. A skilled communicator is able to select key pieces of a complex idea to express in words, sounds, and images to build shared understanding (Levy and Murnane 2004). Skilled communications negotiate positive outcomes with customers, subordinates, and superiors through social perceptiveness, persuasion, negotiation, instruction, and service orientation (Peterson et al. 1999).

3. **Nonroutine problem solving**: A skilled problem solver uses expert thinking to examine a broad span of information, recognize patterns, and narrow the information to reach a diagnosis of the problem. Moving beyond diagnosis to a solution requires knowledge of how the information is linked conceptually and involves metacognition—the ability to reflect on whether a problem-solving strategy is working and to switch to another strategy that is working if the current strategy is not (Levy and Murnane 2004). This ability includes creativity to generate new and innovation solutions, integrate seemingly unrelated information, and entertain possibilities others may miss (Houston 2007).

4. **Self-management and self-development**: Self-management skills include the ability to work remotely, in virtual teams; to work autonomously; and to be self-motivating and self-monitoring. One aspect of self-management is the willingness and ability to acquire new information and skills related to work (Houston 2007).

5. **Systems thinking**: Systems thinking means the ability to understand how an entire system works and how an action, change, or malfunction in one part of the system affects the rest of the system—that is, adopting a "big picture" perspective on work (Houston 2007). Systems thinking includes judgment and decision making, systems analysis, and systems evaluation, as well as abstract reasoning about how the different elements of a work process interact (Peterson et al. 1999).

STEM Programs and 21st-Century Skills

STEM programs should help students develop skills of adaptability by providing learners with experiences that require coping with new approaches to investigations, using new tools and techniques to make observations, and collecting and analyzing data. Programs should include opportunities to work individually and in groups on activities such as laboratories and field studies.

STEM programs can introduce complex communications and social skills as a part of laboratories and investigations. STEM activities would include group work that culminates with the use of evidence to formulate a conclusion or recommendation. Students can be required to process and interpret information and data from a variety of sources. Learners should have to select appropriate evidence and use it to communicate an explanation.

STEM programs should help students develop the abilities of nonroutine problem solving by requiring learners to apply knowledge to scientific questions and design technological problems, identify the mathematical components of a contemporary issue, and use reasoning to link evidence to an explanation. In the process of STEM investigations, learners will be required to reflect on the adequacy of an answer to a question or solution to a problem. Students may be required to think of another investigation or another way to gather data and connect those data with the knowledge of STEM disciplines.

Curriculum materials should include opportunities for students to work on STEM investigations alone and in groups. These investigations would include full inquiries and may require learners to acquire new knowledge and develop new skills as they pursue answers to questions or solutions to problems. These experiences would help students develop self-management and self-development abilities.

One of the most helpful innovations in STEM education would be an emphasis on systems thinking. Even traditional STEM disciplines can be approached as living systems, Earth systems, physical systems, and technological systems. Learners should be required to realize the limits to investigations of systems and describe components, flow of resources, changes in systems and subsystems, and reasoning about interactions at the interface between systems.

AN ADVANCED RESEARCH AND DEVELOPMENT WORKFORCE

Pipeline issues have not gone away, especially for computer scientists, environmental scientists, engineers, and health professionals. In addition, increasing the diversity of individuals in STEM careers remains a central goal that can be addressed in STEM programs. STEM education can contribute to the recruitment and retention of individuals into science- and technology-related careers. Such careers will be the basis for innovations needed for a quality environment, prosperous economy, and healthy society. Table 7.3 summarizes the aim for STEM education.

Innovation and STEM Education

In the 20th century, federal investment in scientific and technological research made substantial innovations that contributed to better health, improved communications, and what has to be counted among the greatest technological and engineering accomplishments in human history—sending men to the Moon and returning them safely. Many of these innovations

Table 7.3. Innovation and STEM Careers

National issue	Innovation
Education theme	An advanced research and development workforce
Advancing the goals of STEM education	Focus on STEM careers to • increase the number and diversity of students in STEM professions, • recruit top students to STEM professions, and • keep individuals in STEM careers.

grew out of the physical sciences. The discoveries by Francis Crick and James Watson, as well as Maurice Wilkins and Rosalind Franklin, in the 1950s influenced many innovations in the latter decades of the 20th century. I am referring to fundamental discoveries in molecular and cellular biology.

Advancements in STEM disciplines have continually accounted for innovations and increases in the U.S. gross domestic product (GDP), an indicator of economic productivity. It also is the case that solutions to many of our local, national, and global challenges will result from advances in STEM disciplines. I refer, for example, to health, energy, environmental quality, natural hazards, and use of natural resources. All of these fields depend on a continued flow of individuals in a professional pipeline from K–12 schools to colleges and universities and, in most cases, to graduate programs. Federal investment in basic research plays the major role in innovation, but the influence of K–12 STEM education must not be ignored.

Innovations and STEM Education

For K–12 STEM education, there are insights worth considering if we wish to contribute an answer to this aspect of the question that leads the chapter. While the physical science had a significant role that the 20th century, it is the life and Earth sciences that may well lead in the 21st century. However, there is a convergence of the sciences with technology, engineering, and mathematics as research and development opens fields such as biomedical engineering, energy technology, engineering hazard mitigations, and STEM approaches to environmentally sustainable systems.

Attaining STEM-related personal and social perspectives and developing innovative discoveries and applications require broader and more integrative educational experience. For example, students could have experiences working fluently and harmoniously across STEM disciplines. K–12 STEM education can and should contribute to such experiences and an understanding of 21st-century careers.

Increasing the Diversity of Students in STEM Professions

According to the U.S. Bureau of Labor and Statistics in 2006, only 9% of the nation's scientific and engineering workforce included African Americans, Hispanics, and Native Americans. In comparison, 30% of the U.S. population included the same minority groups.

One place to begin rebalancing the percentage of minorities with aspirations for STEM professions is in K–12 classrooms. Encouraging active learning and collaboration, investigations of challenging problems, and a strong knowledge in STEM disciplines will help. In addition, there are other practices that have proven helpful—summer programs, early research experiences, academic support, social integration, and mentoring by STEM teachers (Hrabowski 2011).

CONCLUSION

This chapter presents what I suggest is the essential question for individuals providing leadership in STEM education: How can the nation (or state, school district, or classroom) develop a coherent and effective strategy for advancing STEM education to ensure that the United States will have

- a STEM-literate society,
- a deep technical workforce for a 21st-century knowledge economics, and
- an advanced research and development workforce focused on innovation?

The first aim emphasizes STEM literacy. In an effort to move from STEM as a slogan to an educational definition, I propose that STEM literacy refers to an individual's

- knowledge, attitudes, and skills to identify questions and problems in life situations, explain the natural and designed world, and draw evidenced-based conclusions about those STEM-related issues;
- understanding of the characteristic features of STEM disciplines as forms of human knowledge, inquiry, and design;
- awareness of how STEM disciplines shape our material, intellectual, and cultural environments; and
- willingness to engage in STEM-related issues and with the ideas of science, technology, engineering, and mathematics as a constructive, concerned, and reflective citizen.

The second theme of the question centers on development of 21st-century workforce skills, including adaptability, complex communication and social interactions, nonroutine problem solving, self-management, and systems thinking.

Finally, there is the continued need for increased numbers and a diversity of individuals to enter and remain in STEM careers. Here, the national issue is innovation based on research and development.

The remaining chapters will provide some directions and details for how states, districts, and schools can begin answering these questions.

DISCUSSION QUESTIONS

1. What are the essential points of the question posed as central to contemporary STEM education?

2. What is your response to the definition of STEM literacy?

3. What are the 21st-century skills described in this chapter, and how could you imagine their development in the context of STEM education?

4. Innovation has been proposed as a national issue. Assuming it is, what could STEM education do to encourage innovation?

CHAPTER 8

What Is Your Perspective of STEM Education?

As we have seen, the acronym *STEM* began at the National Science Foundation (NSF) as an efficient means to identify and communicate four disciplines. With time, *STEM* began being used in discussions of education policy. Again, the acronym's use generally referred to the quartet of disciplines but the use expanded and became more ambiguous as references included, for example, STEM education, a STEM program, integrative STEM, and STEM initiatives. In the policy arena, a STEM perspective referred to perceived outcomes related to knowledge economies, technical innovations, the basis for businesses and industries to thrive, the competencies for a 21st-century workforce, and national security. The ambiguity of STEM in national policy discussions is understandable and acceptable as a general term referring to four disciplines. Policy makers did not have to consider what STEM might mean for specific K–12 school programs. They only had to consider the general implications of policies for the disciplines. At the state level, there are, among other things, STEM councils, networks, hubs, centers, strategic plans, directors, coordinators, and coalitions. All are undoubtedly helpful, but one has to ask about the various perspectives and implicit definitions from which they are recommending changes in graduation requirements, preservice teacher education, teacher licensure, district curricula, professional development, and classroom practices, not to mention state standards, curricula, instruction, and assessments.

However, as use of the acronym moves from national policies to state and local education, there is a compelling need to clarify the meaning of *STEM* for school districts, and classrooms. In particular, one has to ask questions such as the following:

- What are the connections between STEM education and national priorities?
- What about recent developments in common core standards?
- How do STEM perspectives align with funding for Race to the Top?
- Will STEM be included in the reauthorization of the Elementary and Secondary Education Act (ESEA), also known as No Child Left Behind?
- Does STEM have any place in the Next Generation Science Standards?

As the use of the acronym *STEM* gets closer to school districts and especially classrooms, the requirements for clarity and meaning not only increase, but they become critically urgent as well. That said, I caution against the inclination to look for one definition that is acceptable to all.

STEM PERSPECTIVES

This chapter presents different perspectives of STEM education. The goal is to clarify and not confuse the issue of STEM. These perspectives are based on many discussions, articles, reports, and projects where there is reference to STEM.

STEM Equals Science (or Mathematics).

In this first perspective, the use of the acronym *STEM* only means science, and occasionally a specific discipline such as physics or biology. This use of STEM is most confusing due to the multiple disciplinary orientations contrasted with the single discipline reference. In some cases, the referent may be a discipline other than science or mathematics—for example, "We have a STEM program, and it is Engineering Design" (see Figure 8.1).

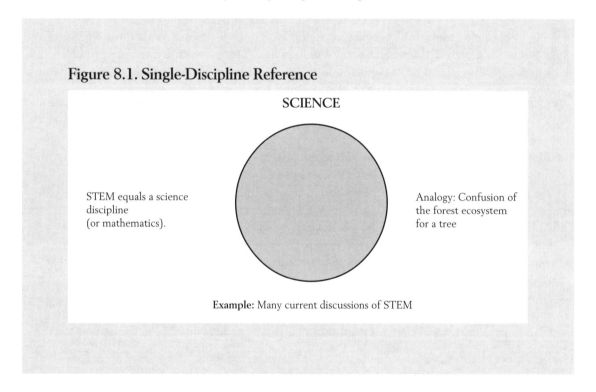

Figure 8.1. Single-Discipline Reference

SCIENCE

STEM equals a science discipline (or mathematics).

Analogy: Confusion of the forest ecosystem for a tree

Example: Many current discussions of STEM

STEM Means Both Science and Mathematics.

In some cases, STEM refers to both science and mathematics. This perspective should not be surprising due to the long history of these disciplines as curricular components in American education. In some discussions of STEM, individuals refer to the separate disciplines as silos. In this perspective, there are silos and postholes (excuse the mixed metaphor). The silos are clearly visible and the postholes are somewhat visible, but the essence of a hole is that there is nothing there; it is empty space, but you know that it is a hole (see Figure 8.2).

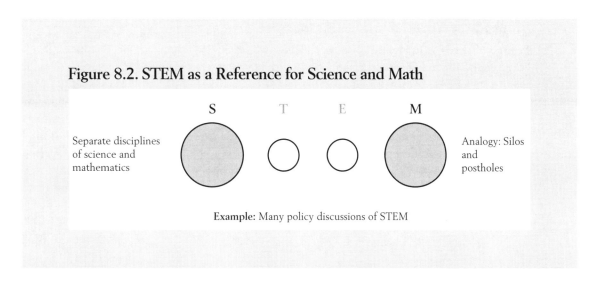

Figure 8.2. STEM as a Reference for Science and Math

STEM Means Science and Incorporates Technology, Engineering, or Math.

Some science teachers incorporate examples of technology and engineering in their lessons. Occasionally elementary teachers introduce engineering and design problems; egg drops are a common example. However, the engineering design is often confused with science practices. This perspective represents the first step toward an integration, but the teacher keeps science (or math) as the dominant discipline and, as appropriate or needed, introduces the other disciplines. As you can imagine, this perspective may have several different variations (e.g., science incorporating technology, science incorporating math, or science incorporating engineering; see Figure 8.3).

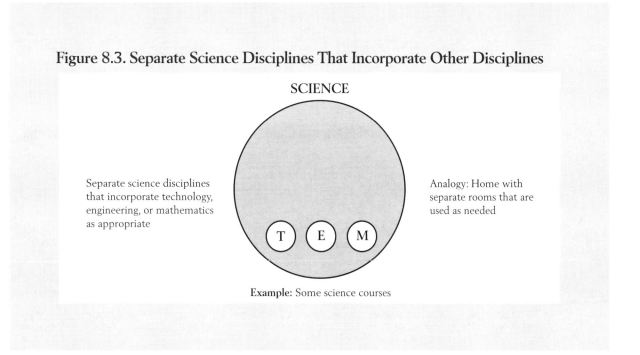

Figure 8.3. Separate Science Disciplines That Incorporate Other Disciplines

The Case for STEM Education

STEM Equals a Quartet of Separate Disciplines.

Let's go back to the metaphor of silos. The reference to STEM in this perspective includes science, technology, engineering, and math, all with places in school curriculum. In some schools, the *T* is included as information technology and the *E* is a course such as Project Lead the Way. This perspective may cover four separate courses or separate units within a course. There are a couple of issues associated with this perspective. If there are three or four separate courses in high school, which ones will be required for graduation? A second issue is the inclusion of technology and engineering. Incorporating separate sections of a course with a title such as Introduction to STEM might be one example. Think of the general science textbooks that had separate units on the science disciplines. So, have the students had ample opportunities to study the respective disciplines (see Figure 8.4)?

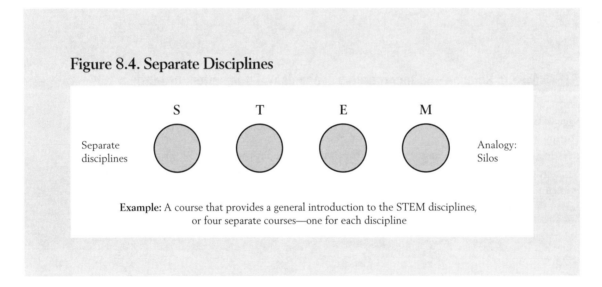

Figure 8.4. Separate Disciplines

Separate disciplines

S   T   E   M

Analogy: Silos

Example: A course that provides a general introduction to the STEM disciplines, or four separate courses—one for each discipline

Although the representation shows the silos as equal, this is not usually the case, especially when requirements for graduation from high school are considered.

STEM Means Science and Math Are Connected by One Technology or Engineering Program.

Science and math are stand-alone disciplines with connections to another program that emphasizes technology and/or engineering. A career and technical education (CTE) program is an example of this perspective of STEM education. Here, individuals will indicate that CTE, for example, is the STEM initiative. The assumption is that science and math already are integral to the school curriculum. One should note that their connection is not necessarily a coordination of concepts and processes of the respective disciplines (see Figure 8.5).

The California project Linked Learning: Pathways to College and Career Success is a very nice example of using technology and engineering projects to connect core subjects of science and math to experiences in professional and technical education in fields such as biomedical

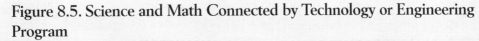

Figure 8.5. Science and Math Connected by Technology or Engineering Program

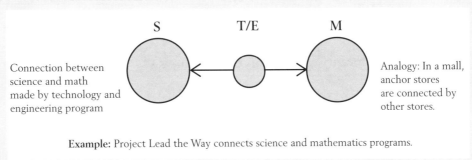

S   T/E   M

Connection between science and math made by technology and engineering program

Analogy: In a mall, anchor stores are connected by other stores.

Example: Project Lead the Way connects science and mathematics programs.

and health sciences, energy resources, information technology, and agriculture. In this example, students also experience work-based learning (Hoachlander and Yanofsky 2011).

STEM Means Coordination Across Disciplines.

We can begin with a common example. Science teachers often ask mathematics teachers to introduce concepts in math that will be applied in science. Less frequently do math teachers ask science or technology teachers to apply math concepts. But in some cases, concepts and processes can be introduced and applied in the different STEM disciplines. Figure 8.6 represents an ideal. In reality, two of the four disciplines likely will coordinate concepts and processes.

Figure 8.6. Coordination Across Disciplines

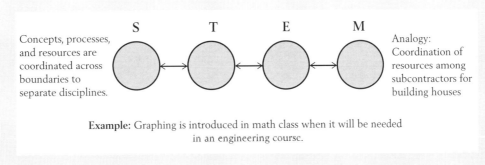

S   T   E   M

Concepts, processes, and resources are coordinated across boundaries to separate disciplines.

Analogy: Coordination of resources among subcontractors for building houses

Example: Graphing is introduced in math class when it will be needed in an engineering course.

STEM Means Combining Two or Three Disciplines.

One form of integration begins by combining two disciplines, such as science and technology or engineering and math. A more complex model combines three of the four disciplines. Integrating science, technology, and math would be an example (see Figure 8.7).

Figure 8.7. Combining Two or Three Disciplines

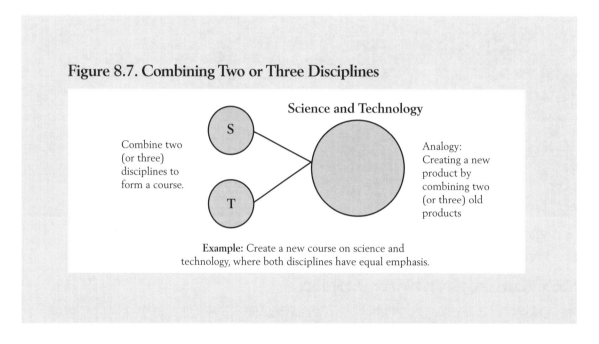

Combine two (or three) disciplines to form a course.

Science and Technology

S

T

Analogy: Creating a new product by combining two (or three) old products

Example: Create a new course on science and technology, where both disciplines have equal emphasis.

STEM Means Complementary Overlapping Across Disciplines.

STEM can be integrated by sequencing disciplines in units or courses, or in lessons so STEM becomes a central emphasis of the education experiences. Figure 8.8 indicates the potential of overlapping STEM disciplines that may occur, for example, in the process of investigating an answer to a scientific question or solving a design problem.

STEM Means a Transdisciplinary Course or Program.

There is a STEM perspective that involves the transdisciplinary approach to major issues such as global climate change, health problems, or use of resources for energy. A course called Sustainable Society might be an example in which the entire group of STEM disciplines, and perhaps others (e.g., ethics, politics, economics), would be used to understand a major contemporary challenge. This perspective could be a senior STEM seminar in which students likely would have taken two or three years of traditional science and math and perhaps a year of technology or engineering (see Figure 8.9).

Figure 8.8. Integrated Disciplines

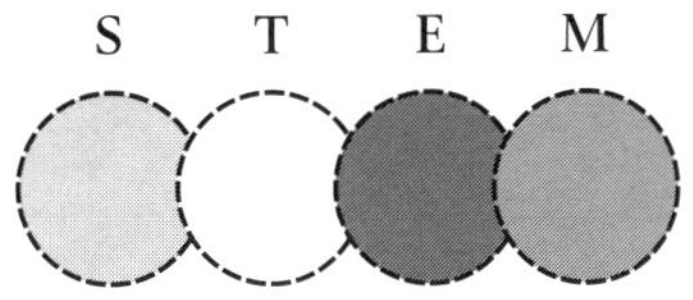

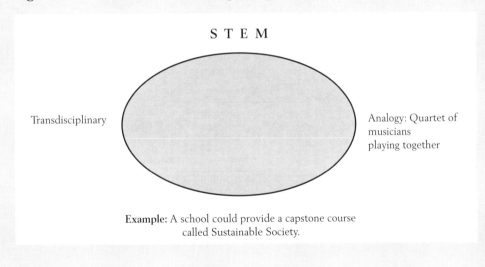

Integrated disciplines through overlapping and sequencing

S   T   E   M

Analogy:
An automobile
manufacturing plant

Example: Students study problems or conduct investigations that overlap and preogress through the disciplines.

Figure 8.9. STEM as a Transdisciplinary Course or Program

S T E M

Transdisciplinary

Analogy: Quartet of
musicians
playing together

Example: A school could provide a capstone course called Sustainable Society.

The Case for STEM Education

CONCLUSION

As one can see, there are many perspectives to STEM education. This chapter presents nine perspectives, and no doubt there are others. My intention is not to present these and then indicate which one is the true STEM perspective. Rather, my intention is to help individuals, organizations, and agencies clarify different perspectives and give insights to those considering or engaged in education reform with a particular STEM perspective.

DISCUSSION QUESTIONS

1. How would you describe your perspective of STEM education?

2. Is there a STEM perspective not described in this chapter? If so, how would you describe it?

3. How would you explain the omission or marginal inclusion of technology and engineering in STEM education?

CHAPTER 9

STEM Education: Where Are You Now, and Where Do You Want to Go?

Many discussions of STEM education begin with a question that assumes curriculum integration is an appropriate approach to reform. This may not be the best question. It may be a better approach to first consider what your system presently does and does not have relative to STEM education. An integrated curriculum may actually be the approach you finally implement. But as you saw in Chapter 8, there are several variations on the integration of STEM disciplines. So, let's begin with these questions: Where are you now? Do you have STEM 1.0? If so, here are the next questions: Where do you want to go? Can you move beyond STEM 1.0 through curriculum reform?

In this chapter, you evaluate the status of STEM education in your state, district, or school; review the different approaches to curriculum, including integration; and begin planning ways to enrich and improve STEM education.

As mentioned in prior chapters, education leaders at state, district, and school levels face the challenge of figuring out what STEM means in the contexts of actual programs of curriculum, instruction, and assessment. This challenge exists at the interface of policies and their realization in terms of educational programs and classroom practices.

To be clear, this chapter does not present a model for STEM programs and practices. My approach begins with opportunities to improve students' overall understanding and achievement in science, technology, engineering, and mathematics education. In short, the aim is to achieve higher levels of STEM literacy. So, my approach here begins by having you look at STEM education as it currently exists in your state, district, or school; determine the potential for reform; and establish directions for change. To accomplish this task, I ask numerous questions designed to advance STEM education within your unique education context.

SURVEYING STEM IN YOUR EDUCATION SYSTEM

The next sections use a contemporary format for asking a question to describe your present situation and proposed future for STEM education. The sections are STEM 1.0 through 4.0 to evaluate STEM education.

Do You Have STEM 1.0?

STEM 1.0 exists when an education system has standards-based K–12 programs for all students in the content areas of science, technology, engineering, and mathematics. In STEM 1.0, the disciplines may be separate. Since the No Child Left Behind (NCLB) legislation, the role of K–12 mathematics has been emphasized, so the likelihood of it not being present is very low, probably zero. But what about science? Since NCLB, the emphasis on science has been reduced in the interest of increased time for language arts and mathematics. Turning to technology and engineering—what is the status for each of these subjects? Use Table 9.1 to briefly describe the status of STEM disciplines in your system.

If you are beginning the journey of STEM education, it is always good idea to know the trip's origin. As when using MapQuest, you have to identify where you are to figure out the details of where you want to go. Table 9.1 presents the opportunity to describe where you are related to the four separate STEM disciplines. For each of the disciplines, briefly describe the current situation for the following categories:

- Curriculum (e.g., fully implemented, locally developed instructional materials)
- Instructional strategies (e.g., use of instructional model in elementary grades and varied strategies in secondary grades)
- Student achievement (e.g., average achievement on state math assessment)
- Strengths (e.g., K–6 teachers have completed a full cycle of professional development)
- Weaknesses (e.g., no engineering curriculum program in middle school and high school)
- Plans (e.g., adopt new mathematics program and professional development for teachers)
- Other comments (e.g., consider alignment with new Common Core State Standards for Mathematics)

One way to think about advancing STEM education is by improving the separate disciplines or incorporating a discipline currently not included, such as engineering. Such an approach maintains the integrity of the traditional disciplines and allows you to move forward with solid, standards-based programs for all K–12 students. Completing the questions for Table 9.1 and appropriate portions of the figures presented in the next section should contribute to this approach.

Are You Considering Curriculum Integration for STEM?

A step beyond maintaining separate STEM disciplines requires consideration and a decision to advance STEM education by integrating the disciplines. This decision can be made at the state level, but in the approach suggested here, the decision is best made at the district or school level.

Several approaches to curriculum integration have been published. I recommend reviewing the following: *Designs for Science Literacy* (AAAS 2000), *Meeting Standards Through Integrated Curriculum* (Drake and Burns 2004), *Making Sense of Integrated Science: A Guide for High Schools* (BSCS 2000), and *Interdisciplinary Curriculum: Design and Implementation* (Jacobs 1989).

Table 9.1. STEM Disciplines

Science and technology education	Science	Technology
Curriculum: Instructional strategies: Student achievement: Strengths: Weaknesses: Plans: Other comments:		
Engineering and mathematics education	Engineering	Mathematics
Curriculum: Instructional strategies: Student achievement: Strengths: Weaknesses: Plans: Other comments:		

Recall the different perspectives of STEM education described in Chapter 8. Here are several variations to consider for the integration of STEM. The first approach maintains STEM 1.0 as a traditional discipline while integrating another STEM discipline. There are several ways this can be done:

- *Coordinate.* Two subjects taught in separate courses are coordinated so content in one subject synchronizes with what is needed in another subject. For example, students in mathematics learn algebraic functions when they need that knowledge in an engineering class.
- *Complement.* While teaching the main content of one subject, the content of another subject is introduced to complement the primary subject. For example, while students are designing an energy-efficient car in a technology class, science concepts of frictional resistance (drag), loss of kinetic energy, and mass are introduced to help them improve the car's design and efficiency.
- *Correlate.* Two subjects with similar themes, content, or processes are taught so students understand the similarities and differences. For example, you might teach scientific practices and engineering design in separate science and technology courses.
- *Connections.* Use one discipline to connect other disciplines, such as using technology as the connection between science and mathematics.
- *Combine.* This approach combines two or more STEM disciplines using projects, themes, procedures, or other organizing foci. For example, one could establish a new course on science and technology that uses student projects to show the relationship between science and technology.

Because of the dominance of the traditional disciplines in state, district, and school standards, curricula, and assessments, it likely will be important for you to provide a rationale supporting recommendations for integrating the STEM disciplines. This is especially the case when you move beyond integration through coordination, complements, correlation, or connections. Combining subjects or designing courses that transcend the separate STEM disciplines will require elaborate justifications. Following are examples of arguments against and for curricular integration of STEM.

The arguments against integration rest on reasonable but not unassailable grounds. One of the first arguments is that specific domains have their own ways of knowing. For example, scientific inquiry and engineering design have different aims and criteria. Another argument is that many integrated approaches historically have lacked rigor and not been standards-based. Finally, understanding domains of inquiry requires an in-depth conceptual foundation (Bransford, Brown, and Cocking 1999; Donovan, Bransford, and Pellegrino 2000). Making connections across disciplines is not as clear and straightforward as many claim.

The arguments for curricular integration include the following. First, the situations of life and living are all integrated. The decisions citizens face are not nicely contained within disciplines such as science or mathematics. Life situations typically require the knowledge, abilities, and skills of multiple disciplines. Second, individuals learn best when the context within which they are learning has personal meaning—that is, learning is enhanced when it is related to something people recognize or know, or in which they have a personal interest. Third, there is an efficiency that comes with combining the knowledge and skills of different disciplines, and there is limited time in school days and years. If lessons, courses, and school programs can attain learning outcomes of both content and processes of different disciplines, such as engineering and mathematics, that has benefit for teachers and students.

How can states, districts, and schools achieve an appropriate balance among the separate STEM disciplines and an integrated approach? This may be the best question. STEM education does not have to be an either/or decision. This view, by the way, is the reason I began the chapter with a discussion of STEM as separate disciplines and recommended strengthening current curricula, most likely the science and mathematics programs, while implementing technology and engineering materials if they are marginal or lacking.

Moving Beyond STEM 1.0 Through Curriculum Integration

After considering the advantages and disadvantages of integrated approaches to STEM education, it is reasonable to review the levels, subjects, and approaches you think are best for your situation. There is no single best approach to STEM education. Different approaches to STEM education have their advantages and disadvantages. What do you want to achieve? What is the best approach to achieve your goals? What is reasonable given your education system?

You might consider an approach that maintains the best of both a discipline-based program and some form of an integrated STEM curriculum. You might be criticized for a middle-ground initiative, but you might be recognized for implementing a reasonable and manageable perspective.

- First, maintain and improve the traditional STEM disciplines. If technology and engineering are weak or lacking, remedy the situation as best you can.
- Second, within the STEM disciplines, find places to coordinate, complement, correlate, and connect the disciplines. I discuss combining disciplines in another section.
- Third, you may find curricular integration easier at the elementary and middle school levels. If so, begin there.
- Fourth, introducing separate STEM disciplines at the high school level will help students develop more sophisticated understanding of the concepts and procedures of STEM disciplines. Proposing integrated courses that address the core ideas and practices of disciplines is an option you might review.
- Fifth, develop integrated units that can be used within the current K–12 curriculum. The units can be used for professional development and as initial steps towards integrated STEM education.

As this discussion and an evaluation of STEM progresses, I fully realize that the approach may be misused due to the fact that some content from one discipline may be found in any other discipline. Can the evaluation be misused? Yes, but it will likely be very helpful for those who want to take an honest look at what currently exists and changes that may be possible. The team of Jo Anne Vasquez, Cary Sneider, and Michael Comer have published a valuable book, *STEM Lesson Essentials: Integrating Science, Technology, Engineering, and Mathematics* (2013), for those wishing to move beyond STEM 1.0 through curriculum integration.

STEM 2.0, 3.0, OR 4.0?

In your system, are there any examples of STEM that are more than the initial STEM 1.0? This section provides a way of thinking about different levels of integration using the four STEM disciplines as organizers.

Do You Have STEM 2.0?

Table 9.2 presents a list of options for the integration of two STEM disciplines. This is only an evaluation of what may exist in your system; it is not a recommendation to have units, courses, or programs for all six possibilities. Briefly indicate the grade level and approach for the appropriate options, such as "science and math, coordinated in 9th grade"; "technology and engineering, combined as an optional course in 11th grade"; "science and technology, combined in elementary school."

Table 9.2. Two Integrated Disciplines: STEM 2.0

STEM disciplines	Coordinated	Complemented	Correlated	Connected	Other
Science and technology					
Science and engineering					
Science and math					
Technology and engineering					
Technology and math					
Engineering and math					

Do You Have STEM 3.0?

Table 9.3 represents an even more integrated approach to STEM education. Again, this is an evaluation to help with your decisions and planning. Indicate the examples of STEM 3.0 that exist in your education system. For example, we have a fully integrated math, technology, and science course for 10th grade.

Table 9.3. Three Integrated Disciplines: STEM 3.0

STEM disciplines	Examples
Science, technology, and engineering	
Science, engineering, and math	
Technology, engineering, and math	
Math, technology, and science	

Do You Have STEM 4.0?

This example represents a full integration of the four STEM disciplines. In Table 9.4, describe the units, courses, or programs for STEM 4.0 in your state, district, or school.

Table 9.4. A STEM 4.0 Program

STEM disciplines	Example
Integrated science, technology, engineering, and math program	

After completing your evaluation of STEM in your education system, you might consider these additional questions, regardless of the STEM 2.0, 3.0, or 4.0 perspectives.

- Do the STEM disciplines have representation at all grades K–12? If not, which grade (or grades) needs attention?
- Do the units, courses, or programs present the concepts and practices of the STEM disciplines with equal focus, rigor, and coherence? If not, what needs to be changed?

CONCLUSION

Most states, districts, and schools have STEM programs, but the depth and quality vary. This chapter takes a basic approach to this issue. I first ask you to clarify the status of the separate disciplines of STEM. Based on the current situation, one approach is to simply improve the separate STEM disciplines or implement new programs if they are not a part of the education system.

A second step in improving STEM education is to move toward integration by coordinating, complementing, correlating, or connecting various disciplines, concepts, processes, themes, or topics between or among STEM disciplines.

Third, there is the possibility of combining two, three, or all four STEM disciplines and implementing an integrated approach to the STEM curriculum.

Improving STEM education can take on different features, ranging from staying with and improving the four disciplines to fully integrating the disciplines. The approach taken in this book does not assume one answer or best approach. That said, there is a need to improve STEM education.

DISCUSSION QUESTIONS

1. What are the advantages and disadvantages of maintaining but improving separate STEM programs?

2. What are the reasons to integrate the STEM disciplines?

3. What are the problems of integrating, designing, and implementing an integrated approach to STEM?

CHAPTER 10

What Is Your Action Plan for STEM Education?

How can you go about improving STEM education in your system? Well, to state the obvious, you will need a plan. Based on your understanding of the status of STEM education and the general goal of improving STEM education, it is a good idea to establish a plan of action. This chapter first addresses the big picture for your plan of action. The second part of the chapter uses an adaptation of the 4Ps—purpose, policies, programs, and practices—to help with a detailed plan for improving STEM education.

Your approach to improving STEM education can be like planning a trip. The first step usually involves understanding the trip's purpose. Establishing some parameters for the trip is a good idea: Where are you going? Why are you going? How much time will you take? How will you travel? Who is going? Involving key people in planning is also important. Once questions such as these are answered and support for the trip is established, you can work out many of the details. As you begin working on the details, some of the initial plans likely will change. It also is the case that once you begin the trip, some element of the plans may change. Your experiences can certainly fill in the details and elaborate on this analogy.

First, the chapter begins with a general discussion of your approach to improving STEM education. I have found this discussion very helpful. Too often, reforms begin with a specific action, "such as adopt new instructional materials," and devotes little or no attention to other actions, such as getting administrative or community support for the changes. I encourage you to take the time to develop the big picture. The second part of the chapter presents an orientation and discussion that center on details for an action plan.

A PLAN OF ACTION FOR STEM REFORM?

Clarifying a plan of action is one important way to think about improving STEM education. How will you bring about and sustain the changes that constitute an improvement in STEM education? To use a common phrase, do you see the improvement as an event or a process? Is the focus of change on a component of the education system or the system itself?

Try this: Create a story about the process of reforming and improving STEM education in your state, district, or school. Table 10.1 (p. 90) will help organize your story.

Table 10.1. Clarifying a Plan of Action for Reforming K–12 STEM Education

Category	Example
Unit of change	School district
Plan of action	Professional development
Critical resources	Budget
Components of change	Curriculum and assessment
Time frame for change	Two years
Support for change	Superintendent of district

The Basis for a Plan of Action

Whether the initiative is STEM education or new national or state standards and assessments, teachers will be concerned about curriculum materials and assessments. If one thinks about economies of supply and demand as a metaphor, STEM education has a surplus of supply-side activities, supplements, and materials and a deficit of demand-oriented responses. That is, numerous individuals have created what they think are important for STEM education—a supply of options. Few have considered the demand from teachers, coordinators, principals, and superintendents. In this chapter, I am taking a demand-side position. The teachers ask about instructional materials, for example, that represent or model the innovations STEM represents.

So, imagine you are going to implement STEM units. What design criteria would you propose? For example, what length of time would the units require? What concepts would be included? What practices would be emphasized? Would assessments be formative? Summative? Both? Given the discussions of STEM 1.0, 2.0, 3.0, and 4.0 in the prior chapter, which orientation would you propose?

How Long Will It Take?

Achieving significant levels of change in STEM education cannot be accomplished quickly. Table 10.2 presents specification for phases and goals for reform centering on advancing STEM education. Your phases and timeline will vary depending on budget, schedules for adoption of instructional materials, professional development programs, and support for reform of state or local polices. Go ahead and fill in the blanks for your education system.

What Is Your "Story" of Improving STEM Education? Here Is an Example.

The primary work of the first phase is creating a plan to establish clear purposes for STEM education. This phase may also include developing policies for selection of instructional materials, professional development, and assessments of STEM. The second phase would focus on introducing little changes with big effects.

The third phase covers "systemic changes that make a difference"—that is, bringing the reform to scale. After the initial phases, efforts to bring the reform to a significant scale become important. Evaluations of teachers' responses and students' achievements, abilities, and attributes also are reviewed and analyzed as part of the third phase. These data form the basis for

Table 10.2. Action: Phases and Goals

Phase	Timeline	Goal
Initiating the STEM education reform		
Implementing the action plan for STEM education		
Bringing the STEM reform to scale		
Sustaining the STEM education reform		
Evaluating the STEM education reform		

revision of the original plan of action. This phase includes major efforts to review and revise policies and standards and create new criteria for adoptions of instructional materials.

This phase likely would present the most difficulty as policy makers and educators directly confront resistance to change and criticisms of the new initiatives and changes in policies, programs, and practices.

The work of sustaining the idea of "building local capacity for a national purpose" is concentrated in the final phase. The work focuses on building local capacity for ongoing improvement of STEM education as the district level. These efforts phase out the use of external funds for the reform effort and phase in school districts' use of resources in response to the continued improvement of STEM and the implied changes for the school programs.

Evaluation involves continuous feedback about the work and the changes in content and curricula, teachers and teachings, and assessment and accountability. Clearly, feedback occurs during all phases for "monitoring and adjusting to change." The feedback informs judgments about the plan and issues associated with its implementation. Evaluations and feedback are conducted and available at appropriate levels.

THE DETAILS OF IMPROVING STEM EDUCATION: FROM PURPOSES TO PRACTICES

When I introduced the 4Ps in my 1997 book *Achieving Scientific Literacy: From Purposes to Practices*, I had several goals:

- Present a systemic view of education reform.

- Describe the scale of education reforms in terms of time, space, materials, constituents, location, duration, and the politics of agreement.
- Accommodate different perspectives—philosophical purposes, education policies, curriculum programs, and classroom practices.

For the most part, the discussions maintained a national perspective and were intended to explain to the reader the different dimensions and difficulties of achieving scientific literacy.

I still think the 4Ps are understandable and useful ways to think about the education system and approaches to reform. So, I have adapted the 4Ps here and introduce them as a way to help you develop a plan for advancing STEM education, regardless of your location in the system—state, district, or school.

What Are the 4Ps?

Let's begin with a brief review of the 4Ps: purpose, policy, program, and practices. Figure 10.1 summarizes the 4Ps.

Figure 10.1. The 4Ps and STEM Education

What Is the *Purpose* of STEM Education?
Purpose statements include the aims, goals and rationale for STEM education. The statements of purpose are broad and identify knowledge, skills, and abilities that students should develop for effective citizenship in the 21st century. Achieving STEM literacy is an example of an encompassing purpose statement.

What *Policies* Will Support STEM Education?
Policies present specific statements for different components of the education system. Policies translate the goals of STEM into content and performance standards, curriculum designs, assessment frameworks, and teacher education programs. Specifications for STEM curriculum and instruction for K–12 in a school district provide an example of policies. State standards for science, technology, engineering, and math also are examples of policies.

What *Programs* Are Needed to Implement STEM Education?
You will need programs and the actual materials, e-books, software, tests, and equipment that are used to implement STEM policies and purpose. STEM programs would be unique to states, districts, and schools as well as grade levels. Curriculum materials for K–6 STEM education and professional development for high school STEM teachers are two examples of programs.

What *Practices* Are Most Appropriate for STEM Education?
Practices are the specific strategies and methods used by STEM teachers. Practices are the unique and most fundamental dimensions of STEM education and are consistent with the purpose, polices, and program. Practices also reflect the teachers' strength and understanding of the school and students.

Dimensions of Your Action Plan

With the 4Ps in mind, you can begin thinking about various dimensions for the improvement of STEM education. Based on the work initiated in the prior chapter, developing an action plan can continue with a consideration of time, participants, location, problems, products, agreement, and budget for the process of improving STEM education. These perspectives are summarized with questions in Table 10.3.

Table 10.3. Reforming Dimension of STEM Education

Perspectives	Time	Participants	Location	Problems	Products	Agreement	Budget
Reforming STEM education in your state, district, or school	How long will it take to reform STEM education in your state, district, or school?	Who will be involved?	Where will the activities occur?	What problems do you anticipate?	What actual products will be produced?	How difficult will it be to reach agreement among participants?	What is the budget? Who is responsible for the budget?

Next, let's move to a process of clarifying the purpose of STEM education. Complete Table 10.4 by briefly describing your estimates of the different dimensions for developing the purpose—that is, aims and goals—of STEM education.

Table 10.4. Developing the Purpose of STEM Education

Perspective	Time	Participants	Location	Problems	Products	Agreement	Budget
Purpose	How long will it take to prepare a statement of goals?	Who will write about aims and goals of STEM education?	Where will meetings and work occur?	What problems do you anticipate in developing new goals for STEM?	What publications, reports, or web notices do you propose?	How will you reach agreement on the goals for STEM?	What is the budget?
• Establishing goals for STEM • Establishing priorities for STEM goals • Providing justification for STEM education							What is the budget? Who is responsible for decisions about the budget?

Table 10.5 uses the same perspective but focuses attention on the development of policies as part of your action plan. Provide responses for the different questions.

Table 10.5. Developing Policies for STEM Education

Perspective	Time	Participants	Location	Problems	Products	Agreement	Budget
Policy	How long will it take to develop frameworks for STEM education?	Who will develop the policy statements and frameworks?	What is the unit of change for STEM education?	Where are there conflicts between current policies and new policies?	Do you propose longer statements of standards, frameworks, and blueprints for STEM education?	How will negotiations, tradeoffs, and revisions be handled?	What is the budget?
• Establishing design criteria for STEM programs • Identifying criteria for STEM instruction • Developing frameworks for STEM curriculum instruction and assessment							What is the budget? Who is responsible for decisions about the budget?

The development of an action plan for STEM programs now becomes much more complex, timely, and expensive. Table 10.6 presents the same perspectives and a series of questions that will help you complete initial development of the programmatic or curricular aspects of your action plan.

Table 10.6. Developing Programs for STEM Education

Perspective	Time	Participants	Location	Problems	Products	Agreement	Budget
Programs	How will the complete STEM education program be developed?	Who will be responsible for designing, developing, and selecting programs?	What is the critical unit of change?	What are the anticipated problems of implementing the program?	Usually several books for students and teachers will be needed.	What requirements will the STEM program meet?	What is the budget? Who is responsible for decisions about the budget?
• Developing materials or adopting a program for STEM • Implementing the STEM program							

Finally, there is a need to establish a plan to change the classroom practices of STEM teachers. Table 10.7 identifies questions that will help you think through some of the important perspectives of this critical phase of improving STEM education.

Table 10.7. Developing Plans to Change Classroom Practices for STEM Education

Perspective	Time	Participants	Location	Problems	Products	Agreement	Budget
Practices	What will it take to complete implementation and staff development for STEM?	Who will work with school personnel to change practices?	How will classroom changes occur?	What problems are anticipated for change practices?	What will be the materials for the STEM programs?	How will unique needs of schools and teachers be accommodated?	What is the budget? Who is responsible for decisions about the budget?
• Changing teaching strategies for STEM • Adapting materials to unique needs of teachers, schools, and students							

Considering the time, participants, location of change, anticipated problems, products, agreement, and budget will serve as a good beginning for the proposed change in STEM education. Clarifying the goals for STEM education and curriculum policies may be relatively short and easy, while adopting or developing a curriculum program and initiating teaching practices will be larger, more difficult, longer, and more expensive.

Purpose statements and general learning outcomes for STEM are, all things considered, relatively easier and require less time. Establishing policies may take a little longer than the goals and rationale for STEM, but educators have standards, benchmarks, and frameworks that contribute to a foundation for STEM education. Changing programs and practices presents the most challenges in time and effort, but this is most essential. The products needed for reform increase in size, cost, and complexity as you move from purpose to practice. STEM programs, whether covering separate disciplines or an integrated curriculum, require laboratory facilities and equipment, student and teacher materials, and various educational technologies. All of this is—to note the obvious—expensive.

All of these perspectives illuminate the issue of reaching political agreement if one wishes to advance STEM education. Developing and publishing new purposes involves a relatively small number of people, and they do not have to reach complete agreement. Agreeing on specific policies for a curriculum is more difficult and often requires political negotiations, along with recognizing and accepting tradeoffs. Adopting new programs for STEM education means considering the national agenda; state frameworks; local syllabi; community priorities; budgets; and most important, teachers' knowledge, skills, and beliefs about STEM education. But the story does not end here. Once an education system agrees on a curriculum program, further issues arise, such as accommodating the needs and concerns of the teachers who must implement the STEM program. School personnel must agree on teaching strategies and on how to accommodate the program and the philosophy inherent in earlier agreements.

This discussion may begin to sound like a reason to not engage in the advancement of STEM education. Rather, it is an attempt to be honest and clear about the dimensions, dynamics, and difficulties that the education leader will face. Let's use the 4Ps and identify some of the difficulties that a leader—you—may face.

Difficulties of STEM Reform

Table 10.8 presents another aspect of STEM reform. The table uses technological terms—*risk*, *cost*, *constraints*, *responsibilities*, and *benefits*—as categories. Moving from the abstract, impersonal scale of national reports to the concrete, personal scale of the classroom, descriptions in the table indicate that vulnerabilities increase dramatically. The responsibilities and requirements of leadership likewise increase. Educators outside the classroom place a tremendous burden on teachers, often with little recognition of their needs and little support for the tremendous changes required. It is incumbent on every educator who is not in a K–12 STEM classroom to support those who are ultimately responsible for improving STEM education—the teachers. Table 10.8 assumes that the new purposes in the many reports from business and industry will be transformed into policies, programs, and eventually practices. The difficulties increase as these transformations reach STEM classrooms, the critical level of any reform. Interestingly, the benefits to students become clear as one implements change at the level of practices. Take a few minutes and, to the best of your knowledge, answer the questions in Table 10.8.

Table 10.8. Difficulties of STEM Reform

Perspective	What is the risk to individual school personnel?	What is the cost to the state, district, or school in financial terms?	What are the constraints against reform for the state, district, or school?	What are the responsibilities of the state, district, or school personnel for reform?	What are the benefits to school personnel and students?
Purpose					
• Establishing goals for STEM					
• Establishing priorities for STEM					
• Providing justification for STEM					
Policy					
• Establishing design criteria for STEM programs					
• Identifying criteria for STEM instruction					
• Developing frameworks for STEM curriculum, instruction, and assessment					

Table 10.8. *(continued)*

Perspective	What is the risk to individual school personnel?	What is the cost to the state, district, or school in financial terms?	What are the constraints against reform for the state, district, or school?	What are the responsibilities of the state, district, or school personnel for reform?	What are the benefits to school personnel and students?
Program					
• Developing materials or adopting a program for STEM					
• Implementing for STEM program					
Practices					
• Changing teaching strategies for STEM					
• Adapting STEM materials to the unique needs of states, schools, and students					

Individual perspectives on STEM education can be constrained by professional responsibilities. For STEM teachers, these responsibilities might be the practical requirements of classroom life, and for others, the perspective is that of curriculum development or state bureaucracies. We need leadership at all these levels from those in a position to translate and adapt purposes to policies, polices to programs, and programs to practices. Teacher educators are key leaders in this process of adaptation. State supervisors, district coordinators, assessment specialists, professional developers, and school administrators function in ways that monitor and regulate the process of STEM reform across boundaries, reduce constraints, and provide support and feedback for innovative practices. These leaders work to articulate the purposes, policies, programs, and practices of science, technology, engineering, and mathematics education.

CONCLUSION

The frameworks described in this chapter provide a useful means for developing an action plan and monitoring the progress in transforming STEM education. You can begin with a general and strategic plan of action and, among other things, gain support for the plan. Then you can move on to the details of clarifying the purpose of STEM, establishing policies for curriculum programs, adopting the programs, and providing professional development to establish instructional practices. Is the education system spending more time, money, and effort on developing its goal statement or implementing the new STEM programs? At the state level, is funding concentrated on policy statements or various curriculum materials and professional development programs? Many of the documents and reports that form the basis for improving STEM education indicate a considerable effort at the policy level. Now it is time to address the dimensions of reforming programs and practices and recognize the difficulties of STEM reform at these levels.

DISCUSSION QUESTIONS

1. What do you perceive as the basic problem of going from purposes to practices in STEM education?

2. What is the elevator speech (2–3 minutes) for your action plan to improve STEM education?

3. How would you describe the work of individuals at the interface of two of the 4Ps—for example, working to translate STEM policy to actual programs or translating curriculum programs to classroom practices?

4. From your perspective, which means of improving STEM education has the highest probability of success in your education system? Explain why.

CONCLUSION

The acronym *STEM* is ubiquitous on the education landscape. As such, the meaning of STEM varies with contexts as different individuals use the acronym. So, let's begin this conclusion by establishing at least one meaning for STEM—in particular, STEM literacy. The following meaning was stated in the introduction, and I provide it again here. STEM literacy refers to an individual's

- knowledge, attitudes, and skills to identify questions and problems in life situations, explain the natural and designed world, and draw evidence-based conclusions about STEM-related issues;
- understanding of the characteristic features of STEM disciplines as forms of human knowledge, inquiry, and design;
- awareness of how STEM disciplines shape our material, intellectual, and cultural environments; and
- willingness to engage in STEM-related issues and with the ideas of science, technology, engineering, and mathematics as a constructive, concerned, and reflective citizen.

Having addressed one of the major challenges of STEM education, establishing the purposes of STEM, we can move on to other challenges and opportunities.

The United States needs a broader, more coordinated strategy for precollege education in science, technology, engineering, and mathematics (STEM). That strategy should include all the STEM disciplines and address the need for greater diversity in the STEM professions, a workforce with deep technical and personal skills, and a STEM-literate citizenry prepared to address the grand challenges of the 21st century. There have been repeated efforts to produce major improvements in such education. More than 50 years ago, the United States engaged in a massive effort to improve science education in order to win a race to space. The chief competitor was clear: the Soviet Union. The primary goal was clear: Send men to the Moon. And the timeline was clear: by the end of the decade.

Now the United States must address the reform of STEM education, in this case because we are losing our competitive edge in the global economy. However, this era is very different from the Sputnik era. The competitors are greater in number—countries with developed

Conclusion

economies, such as Canada, France, Germany, and Japan, and especially the fastest-growing economies, such as China and India. The primary goal is less clear and more complex: to prosper in a global economy and maintain national security. The timeline for achievement is less clear: a decade? A half century? Finally, the perception of the relationship among the four disciplines of STEM continues to be unclear.

For many, STEM means only science and mathematics, even though the products of technology and engineering have so greatly influenced everyday life. A true STEM education should increase students' understanding of how things work and improve their use of technologies. STEM education should also introduce more engineering during precollege education. Engineering is directly involved in problem solving and innovation, two themes with high priority on every nation's agenda. Given its relation to a knowledge economy, students should learn about engineering and develop some of the skills and abilities associated with the design process. The good news is that the National Assessment Governing Board (NAGB) has recognized the importance of this issue and recently approved the evaluation of technology and engineering literacy through an assessment that will be given to U.S. students in 2014. Likewise, the framework for the Next Generation Science Standards released by the National Academies in 2013 includes technology and engineering. There are also standards for technological literacy (ITEA 2000). Finally, the Next Generation Science Standards include engineering.

As stressed in several reports on a deep technical workforce for the 21st century, students must acquire skills such as adaptability, complex communication and social skills, nonroutine problem solving, self-management, and systems thinking to compete in the modern economy. To the degree that STEM curricula incorporate group activities, laboratory investigations, and projects, they will afford students the opportunity to develop these essential 21st-century skills and prepare them to become citizens who are better able to make decisions about personal health, energy efficiency, environmental quality, resource use, and national security. Indeed, the competencies that citizens need to understand and address such issues, from the personal to global perspectives, are as clearly linked to knowledge in STEM disciplines as they are to economics, politics, and cultural values.

The STEM community responded vigorously to produce the Sputnik-spurred education reforms of the 1960s. Likewise, the United States needs a bold new mission and strategy for improving education that includes the development of high-quality teachers, effective instruction, and curriculum materials with grand challenges of society at the center of study. It is time to move beyond slogans and make STEM literacy a reality for all students.

REFERENCES

Afterschool Alliance. 2011. *STEM learning in afterschool: An analysis of impact and outcomes.* Washington, DC: Afterschool Alliance.

American Association for the Advancement of Science (AAAS). 1989. *Science for all Americans: A project 2061 report on goals in science, mathematics, and technology.* Washington, DC: AAAS.

American Association for the Advancement of Science (AAAS). 1993. *Benchmarks for science literacy.* New York: Oxford University Press.

American Assocation for the Advancement of Science (AAAS). 2000. *Designs for science literacy.* New York: Oxford University Press.

Angier, N. *New York Times.* 2010. STEM Education Has Little to Do With Flowers. October 4.

Atkin, J. M., and P. Black. 2003. *Inside science education reform: A history of curricular and policy change.* New York: Teachers College Press.

Barney, G. 1980. *The global 2000 report to the president: Entering the twenty-first century.* Washington, DC: U.S. Government Printing Office.

Beberman, M. 1958. *An emerging program of secondary school mathematics.* Cambridge, MA: Harvard University Press.

Bestor, A. 1953. *Educational wastelands: The retreat from learning in our public schools.* Urbana, IL: University of Illinois Press.

Biological Sciences Curriculum Study (BSCS). 2000. *Making sense of integrated science: A guide for high schools.* Colorado Springs: BSCS.

Biological Sciences Curriculum Study (BSCS). 2007. *A decade of action: Sustaining global competitiveness.* Colorado Springs: BSCS.

Board on Science Education (BOSE). 2013. *Monitoring progress toward successful K–12 STEM education: A nation advancing?* Washington, DC: National Academies Press.

Bransford, J. D., A. L. Brown, and R. R. Cocking. 1999. *How people learn: Brain, mind, experience, and school.* Washington, DC: National Academies Press.

References

Brown, L. 1981. *Building a sustainable society.* New York: W. W. Norton & Company.

Brown, L. 2001. *Eco-economy: Building an economy for the Earth.* New York: W. W. Norton & Company.

Brown, L. 2008. *Plan B 3.0: Mobilizing to save civilization.* New York: W. W. Norton & Company.

Brown, R., J. Brown, R. Reardon, and C. Merrill. 2011. Understanding STEM: Current perceptions. *The Technology and Engineering Teacher* 70 (6): 5–9.

Brown, L., J. Larsen, and B. Fischlowitz-Roberts. 2002. *The Earth policy reader.* New York: W. W. Norton & Company.

Bruner, J. 1960. *The process of education.* New York: Vantage Books.

Bybee, R. W. 1993. *Reforming science education: Social perspectives and personal reflections.* New York: Teachers College Press.

Bybee, R. W. 1997a. *Achieving scientific literacy: From purposes to practices.* Portsmouth, NH: Heinmann.

Bybee, R. W. 1997b. The Sputnik era: Why is this educational reform different from all other reforms? Prepared for the symposium Reflecting on Sputnik: Linking the Past, Present, and Future of Educational Reform, Center for Science, Mathematics, and Engineering Education, National Research Council, Washington, DC. *www.nas.edu/sputnik/bybee1.htm*

Bybee, R. W. 2010. *The teaching of science: 21st-century perspectives.* Arlington, VA: NSTA Press.

Bybee, R. W. 2011. Scientific and engineering practices in K–12 classrooms: Understanding a framework for K–12 science education. *The Science Teacher* 78 (9): 34–40.

Bybee, R. W., and B. McCrae, eds. 2009. *PISA science 2006: Implications for science teachers and teaching.* Arlington, VA: NSTA Press.

Carroll, L. (1872) 1999. *Through the looking glass and what Alice found there.* Reprint, Mineola, NY: Dover Publications.

Carson, R. 1962. *Silent spring.* Boston, MA: Houghton Mifflin.

Center for American Progress (CAP). 2011. *Slow off the mark: Elementary school teachers and the crisis in science, technology, engineering, and math education.* Washington, DC: CAP.

Cremin, L. 1961. *The genius of American education.* New York: Vintage.

Cremin, L. 1976. *Public education.* New York: Basic Books.

DeBoer, G. E. 1991. *A history of ideas in science education: Implementation or practice.* New York: Teachers College, Columbia University.

Donovan, M. S., and J. D. Bransford, eds. 2005. *How students learn: Science in the classroom.* Washington, DC: National Academies Press.

Donovan, S. M., J. D. Bransford, and J. S. Pellegrino, eds. 2000. *How people learn: Bridging research and practice.* Washington, DC: National Academies Press.

Dow, P. 1991. *Schoolhouse politics.* Cambridge, MA: Harvard University Press.

Drake, S. M., and R. C. Burns. 2004. *Meeting standards through integrated curriculum.* Alexandria, VA: Association for Supervision and Curriculum Development (ASCD).

Duncan, A. 2011. Science education and the knowledge economy. *NSTA Reports* (May). *www.nsta.org/publications/news/story.aspx?id=58446*

Educational Policies Commission. 1944. *Education for all American youth.* Washington, DC: National Education Association (NEA).

Ehrlich, P. 1968. *The population bomb.* New York: Ballantine Books.

Elmore, R. 2009. Improving the instructional core. In *Instructional rounds in education: A network approach to improving teaching and learning,* ed. E. U. City, R. Elmore, S. Fiarman, and L. Teite, 249. Cambridge, MA: Harvard Education Press.

Engineering Concepts Curriculum Project (ECCP). 1971. *The man made world.* Columbus, OH: McGraw-Hill.

Entertainment and Media Communications Institute (E&MCI). 2010. *The perception of STEM: Analysis, issues and future directions.* Reston, VA: Entertainment Industries Council, Inc.

Epstein, D., and R. Miller. 2011. *Slow off the mark: Elementary school teachers and the crisis in science, technology, engineering, and math education.* Washington, DC: Center for American Progress.

Fensham, P. 2009. Real-world contexts in PISA science: Implications for context-based science education. *Journal of Research in Science Teaching* 46 (8): 884–896.

Fullan, M. 2001. *The new meaning of educational change.* 3rd ed. New York: Teachers College Press.

Goodman, P. 1964. *Compulsory mis-education.* New York: Horizon Press.

Greenspan, A. 2000. The economic importance of improving math-science education. Testimony before the United States House of Representatives, Committee on Education and the Workforce, September 21. *www.federalreserve.gov/BOARDDOCS/TESTIMONY/2000/20000921.htm*

Gross, R., and J. Murphy, eds. 1964. *The revolution in the schools.* New York: Harcourt, Brace & World.

Hall, G., and S. Hord. 1987. *Change in schools: Facilitating the process.* Albany: State University Press of New York Press.

Hall, G., and S. Hord. 2001. *Implementing change: Patterns, principles, and potholes.* Needham, MA: Allyn and Bacon.

Hardin, G. 1968. The tragedy of the commons. *Science* 162: 1243.

Harris Interactive. 2011. STEM perceptions: Student and parent study. Survey commissioned by Microsoft. *www.harrisinteractive.com*

Harvard Graduate School of Education. 2011. *Pathways to prosperity: Meeting the challenges of preparing young Americans for the 21st century.* Cambridge, MA: Pathways to Prosperity Project.

References

Helgeson, S. L., P. E. Blosser, and R. W. Howe. 1977. *The status of pre-college science, mathematics, and social science education: 1955–1975, Volume I.* Columbus, OH: Center on Science and Mathematics Education, Ohio State University.

Hentoff, N. 1966. *Our children are dying.* Gouldsboro, ME: The Gestalt Journal Press.

Hoachlander, G., and D. Yanofsky. 2011. Making STEM real. *Educational Leadership* 68 (6): 60–65.

Holbrook, J. 2009. Meeting challenges to sustainable development through science and technology education. *Science Education International* 20 (1/2): 44–59.

Holdren, J. P. 2008. Science and technology for sustainable well-being. *Science* 319: 424–434.

Holt, J. 1964. *How children fail.* New York: Pittman Publishing Company.

Houston, J. 2007. Future skill demands: From a corporate consultant perspective. Presentation at the Workshop on Research Evidence Related to Future Demands, National Academies of Science, Washington, DC. *http://www7.nationalacademies.org/cfe/Future_Skill_Demands_Presentations.html*

Hrabowski, F. 2011. Boosting minorities in science. *Science* 331: 125.

Interactive Educational Systems Design, Inc. 2011. *2011 national survey on STEM education: Educator edition. www.learning.com/gostem*

International Technology Education Association (ITEA). 2000. *Standards for technological literacy: Content for the study of technology.* Reston, VA: ITEA.

Jackson, S. A. 2005. The nexus: Where science meets society. *Science* 310: 1634–1639.

Jacobs, G. H. 1989. *Interdisciplinary curriculum: Design and implementation.* Alexandria, VA: Association for Supervision and Curriculum Development (ASCD).

Keefe, B. 2010. *The perception of STEM: Analysis, issues and future directions.* Entertainment and Media Industries Council.

Kennedy, J. F. 1961. Special message by the president on urgent national needs before a joint session of Congress, May 25.

Kozol, J. 1967. *Death at an early age.* Boston, MA: Houghton Mifflin.

Lemke, M., A. Sen, E. Pahlke, L. Partlow, D. Miller, T. Williams et al. 2004. *International outcomes of learning in mathematics literacy and problem solving: PISA 2003 results from the U.S. perspective (NCES 2005-003).* Washington, DC: National Center for Education Statistics, Department of Education.

Levy, F., and R. Murnane. 2004. *The new division of labor: How computers are creating the next job market.* Princeton, NJ: Princeton University Press.

Lichtenberg, J., C. Woock, and M. Wright. 2008. *Ready to innovate.* New York: The Conference Board.

Lomborg, B., ed. 2004. *Global crises, global solutions.* Cambridge, UK: Cambridge University Press.

McCarthy, J. J. 2009. Reflections on our planet and its life, origins, and futures. *Science* 326: 1646–1655.

Meadows, D. 2008. *Thinking in systems.* White River Junction, VT: Chelsea Green Publishing.

National Academy of Engineering (NAE). 2012. The grand challenges of engineering. *www. engineeringchallenges.org*

National Assessment Governing Board (NAGB). 2010. *NAEP technology and engineering framework.* Washington, DC: NAGB.

National Center on Time & Learning (NCTL). 2011. *Strengthening science education: The power of more time to deepen inquiry and engagement.* Boston, MA: NCTL.

National Governors Association (NGA). 2011. *Building a science, technology, engineering, and math education agenda. An update of state actions.* Washington, DC: NGA Center for Best Practices.

National Research Council (NRC). 1996. *National science education standards.* Washington, DC: National Academies Press.

National Research Council (NRC). 2006. *America's lab report: Investigations in high school science.* Washington, DC: National Academies Press.

National Research Council (NRC). 2007a. *Rising above the gathering storm: Energizing and employing America for a brighter future.* Washington, DC: National Academies Press.

National Research Council (NRC). 2007b. *Taking science to school: Learning and teaching science in grades K–8.* Washington, DC: National Academies Press.

National Research Council (NRC). 2008. *Research on future skill demands: A workshop summary.* Washington, DC: National Academies Press.

National Research Council (NRC). 2009. *A new biology for the 21st century.* Washington, DC: National Academies Press.

National Research Council (NRC). 2010. *Exploring the intersection of science education and 21st century skills.* Washington, DC: National Academies Press.

National Research Council (NRC). 2011. *Successful K–12 STEM education: Identifying effective approaches in science, technology, engineering, and mathematics.* Washington, DC: National Academies Press.

National Research Council (NRC). 2012. *Education for life and work: Developing transferable knowledge and skills in the 21st century.* Washington, DC: National Academies Press.

Office of Science and Technology Policy (OSTP). 2011. *Description of 5-year federal STEM education strategies plan: Report to Congress.* Washington, DC: National Science and Technology Council.

Omenn, G. S. 2006. Grand challenges and great opportunities in science, technology, and public policy. *Science* 314: 1696–1704.

Organisation for Economic Cooperation and Development (OECD). 2006. *Assessing scientific, reading, and mathematical literacy: A framework for PISA 2006.* Paris: OECD.

Organisation for Economic Cooperation and Development (OECD). 2009a. *Green at fifteen: How 15-year-olds perform in environmental science and geoscience in PISA 2006.* Paris: OECD.

References

Organisation for Economic Cooperation and Development (OECD). 2009b. *Jobs for youth.* Paris: OECD.

Organisation for Economic Cooperation and Development (OECD). 2009c. *Learning for jobs.* Paris: OECD.

Perrings, C., S. Naeem, F. Ahrestani, D. Bunker, P. Burkill, G. Canziani, and W. Weisser. 2010. Ecosystem services for 2010. *Science* 330: 323.

Peterson, N., M. Mumford, W. Borman, P. Jeannert, and E. Fleishmann. 1999. *An occupational information system for the 21st century: The development of O*Net.* Washington, DC: American Psychological Association.

President's Council of Advisors on Science and Technology (PCAST). 2010. *Prepare and inspire: K–12 science, technology, engineering, and math (STEM) education for America's future.* Office of Science and Technology Policy, Executive Office of the President, Washington, DC.

President's Council of Advisors on Science and Technology (PCAST). 2012. *Engage to excel: Producing one million additional college graduates with degrees in science, technology, engineering, and mathematics.* Washington, DC: Executive Office of the President of the United States.

Public Agenda. 2010. *Are we beginning to see the light?* Washington, DC: Public Agenda.

Pulakos, E. D., S. Arad, M. A. Donnovan, and K. E. Plamondon. 2000. Adaptability in the workplace: Development of taxonomy of adaptive performance. *Journal of Applied Psychology* 81: 612–662.

Ravitch, D. 1983. *The troubled crusade: American education 1945–1980.* New York: Basic Books.

Rischard, J. 2002. *High noon: 20 global problems, 20 years to solve them.* New York: Basic Books.

Rudolph, J. 2002. *Scientists in the classroom: The Cold War reconstruction of American science education.* New York: Palgrave.

Sachs, J. 2004. Sustainable development. *Science* 304: 649.

Sanders, M. 2009. STEM, STEM education, STEM mania. *The Technology Teacher* 68 (4): 20–26.

Scheffler, I. 1960. *The language of education.* Springfield, IL: Thomas

Schwab, J. J. 1958. The teaching of inquiry. *Bulletin of the Atomic Scientists* 14: 374–379.

Schwab, J. J. 1966. *The teaching of science.* Cambridge, MA: Harvard University Press.

Schwab, J. J. 1978a. Education and the structure of the disciplines. In *Science, curriculum, and liberal education: Selected essays*, ed. I. Westbury and N. J. Wilkof, pp. 229–274. Chicago: University of Chicago Press.

Schwab, J. J. 1978b. The practical: A language for curriculum. In *Science, curriculum, and liberal education: Selected essays*, ed. I. Westbury and N. J. Wilkof, pp. 287–321. Chicago: University of Chicago Press.

Schwab, J. J. 1978c. The practical: Translation into curriculum. In *Science, curriculum, and liberal education: Selected essays*, ed. I. Westbury and N. J. Wilkof, pp. 365–383. Chicago: University of Chicago Press.

Shymansky, J. A., W. C. Kyle, and J. M. Alport. 1983. The effects of new science curricula on student performance. *Journal of Research in Science Teaching* 20 (5): 387–404.

United States Commission on National Security/21st Century. 2001. *Road map for national security: Imperative for change.* Washington, DC: U.S. Government Printing Office.

United States Congress. 1958. *The National Defense Education Act of 1958.* Washington, DC: U.S. Government Printing Office.

Vasquez, J., C. Sneider, and M. Comer. 2013. *STEM lesson essentials: Integrating science, technology, engineering, and mathematics.* Portsmouth, NH: Heinemann.

Weiss, I. 1978. *Report of the 1977 national survey of science, mathematics, and social studies education.* Washington, DC: U.S. Government Printing Office.

INDEX

*Page numbers printed in **boldface** type refer to tables or figures.*

Index

Index

The Case for STEM Education

Index

recruitment and preparation of, 42, 43
    elementary teachers, 46–47
The Teaching of Science: 21st-Century Perspectives, vii, 4, 25, 56
Technical Education Resource Center (TERC), 19
Technologists, preparing next generation of, 50–51, 64
Technology
    curricula in Sputnik era, 14, 19
    inclusion in STEM programs, ix, 3, 7, 27–28, 102
    in perspectives of STEM education, **75–79,** 75–80
Timeline for STEM education reform, **8–9, 93–95,** 102
Transdisciplinary STEM education, 78, **79.** *See also* Curricular integration for STEM education
Trends in International Mathematics and Science Study (TIMSS), 47
21st-century workforce skills, x, xii, 33, 34, 37–39, 40, 58, 66–71, 101–102

adaptability, 38, **67,** 68, 102
of advanced research and development workforce, 68–70, **69**
complex communications and social skills, 38–39, **67,** 68, 102
of deep technical workforce, 38, 66–68, **67,** 102
increasing diversity of students in STEM professions, 69–70
innovation, 45, 68–69, **69,** 71
intellectual skills, 37–38
nonroutine problem solving, 39, **67,** 68, 102
pathways to prosperity, 45–46
self-management and self-development, 39, **67,** 68, 102
STEM education and, x, xii, 33, 34, 37–39, **66,** 66–71
to sustain global competitiveness, 42, 46, 51
systems thinking, 39, **67,** 68, 102

U
United Nations Educational, Scientific and Cultural Organization (UNESCO), 37
University of Illinois Arithmetic Project, 14
University of Illinois Committee for School Mathematics (UICSM), 13, 14
University of Maryland Mathematics Project (UMMaP), 14

V
Vasquez, Jo Anne, 85

W
Watson, James, 69
Wilkins, Maurice, 69
Work-based learning, 46
Workforce skills. *See* 21st-century workforce skills
Worldwatch Institute, 35

Z
Zacharias, Jerrold, 13